GOLF'S ULTIMATE EIGHTEEN

GOLF'S ULTIMATE EIGHTEEN

ARNOLD PALMER, JACK NICKLAUS, AMY ALCOTT, AND OTHER GOLF GREATS

Reveal Favorite Holes to Create the Ultimate Fantasy Course

SELLERS
PUBLISHING

by Steve Eubanks

Published by Sellers Publishing, Inc.

161 John Roberts Road, South Portland, Maine 04106

For ordering information:

(800) 625-3386 toll free

(207) 772-6814 fax

Visit our Web site: www.sellerspublishing.com

Email: rsp@rsvp.com

Library of Congress Control Number: 2010920882

ISBN: 978-1-4162-0580-7

Printed in China

Design: Samantha Caplan

Editorial: Kjersti Egerdahl

Image Research: Chris Campbell

Production Coordination: Leah Finger

10 9 8 7 6 5 4 3 2 1

becker&mayer! Books

11120 NE 33rd Place, Suite 101

Bellevue, Washington 98004

www.beckermayer.com

CONTENTS

INTRODUCTION

The most amazing golf courses are like symphonies with eighteen movements, each hole expanding the composer's unique vision.

Such great golf courses have memorable holes. This may sound simplistic, but every designer throughout history has looked for the one or two holes on their courses that would stand out and stand up to the test of time — not just picturesque holes or holes that are impossibly difficult, but holes that create drama; holes that can be the turning point in an average round or a major championship. Because high-caliber golfers have a myriad of opinions about the courses they play, there's not necessarily just one answer to the question: *What makes a particular course great?* There will certainly be differences of opinion about what makes one course universally celebrated while another earns nothing more than a shrug.

Of course, not every hole on a great course is great, but all legendary courses have a few spectacular holes, the kind of holes where history has been made or will be made, and where those who walk the fairways do so with goose bumps on their arms. *Golf's Ultimate Eighteen* is a collection of awe-inspiring holes, composed of the greatest 1st hole from a legendary course, the finest 2nd hole from another, the best 3rd hole from yet another magnificent course, and so on until you have golf's ultimate fantasy course, eighteen memorable pieces strung together to create a dream course every golfer in the world would love to play.

In this book, we have assembled a who's who of golf luminaries, with each discussing his or her favorite hole and revealing what makes it unforgettable. They're able to demystify each hole as they walk readers through their own strategic approaches and personal memories. Jerry Pate describes one of the greatest shots of his career on the most famous par-3 in the world, the 16th at Cypress Point; Tom Weiskopf recounts one of the most historic moments in the game at the celebrated Postage Stamp 8th at Royal Troon; David Graham considers what makes the 6th at Royal Melbourne so challenging; and Jack Nicklaus tells of the genius of the Road Hole 17th at St. Andrews. These are the stories and storytellers that bring great golf holes to life. Sit back and join the most knowledgeable people in the game as they offer lively, illuminating analyses of the holes that have challenged them to accomplish — and even surpass — their own estimable personal bests.

ABOVE: *A view from behind the green on the 6th hole of the Composite Course at Royal Melbourne Golf Club, Australia.* **OPPOSITE:** *An aerial view of the dramatic 16th hole at Cypress Point Club in Monterey, California.*

CHERRY HILLS COUNTRY CLUB
1st Hole

ARNOLD PALMER

Arnold Palmer is The King. No one has had more impact on the game, and no professional athlete has remained so universally revered. Jack Nicklaus and Tiger Woods have won more majors and more titles, but no one has influenced and inspired more golfers than Arnold Palmer. With ninety-two worldwide victories and seven major championship titles, Palmer was an inaugural inductee into the World Golf Hall of Fame. One of his many great moments came during the U.S. Open at Cherry Hills in Denver, Colorado.

"[The first hole at Cherry Hills is] a great opening hole, at least I think so. It certainly did a lot for me. Back then, in 1960, it played about 315 yards, but it was a little downhill, and at 5,000 feet [above sea level] it played even shorter. You've got to understand, a 300-yard tee shot in those days was very unusual with the equipment we had, but I figured I only needed to hit it about 270 yards to reach that green, which was about my average. And I was considered a long hitter. With wooden drivers and balata balls, the average tee shot on tour was only about 250 to 260 yards.

"There was a little bit of an overhang with the tree on the right, but not enough to prevent you from getting the ball up there. In two practice rounds, I'd driven the green without much trouble, so I went into the tournament with that as my game plan. Drive the first, make birdie, and get off to a good start. Then I promptly pushed the ball into the creek in the first round. It had been a dry ditch until the USGA pumped water into it for effect. By the time I got to my ball it had floated down to the green, so I told [USGA executive director] Joe Dey that I would just wait until it got

---

"I SORT OF TOOK MY FRUSTRATIONS OUT ON THAT FIRST TEE SHOT. I KNEW I'D HIT IT GOOD THE SECOND IT LEFT THE CLUB. THE BALL ROLLED ONTO THE FRONT EDGE OF THE GREEN, AND I WAS ABLE TO 2-PUTT FOR BIRDIE. THAT GOT ME GOING, AND I SHOT 65, WHICH, AT THE TIME, WAS THE LOWEST FINAL ROUND IN U.S. OPEN HISTORY."

—ARNOLD PALMER

---

pin high and take a drop from there. Joe didn't much appreciate the joke. He let me know pretty quickly that I would be taking a drop where the ball crossed the margin of the hazard, which was back toward the tee a good many yards. I made a double bogey from there.

"I didn't make the green in the second round either, but I did make a par. Then on Saturday morning — remember, we played the final thirty-six holes on Saturday back then — I finally hit the shot I wanted, but it rolled to the right of the green and got into the high rough, which was tough. I didn't hit a good chip, and 3-putted for bogey. That didn't make me very happy. At the lunch break I was seven shots behind [Mike] Souchak, but I'd

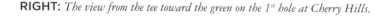

RIGHT: *The view from the tee toward the green on the 1ˢᵗ hole at Cherry Hills.*

played the 1st hole 3-over when I figured I could have played it 3-under. That was six of the seven shots right there.

"I was eating a hamburger and thinking about what I needed to shoot to have a chance of winning when Bob Drum [Pittsburgh journalist and noted curmudgeon who had covered Palmer since high school] in essence told me that I had no chance of winning. I said, 'Well, what if I shoot 65? Two-eighty always wins the Open.' Drum kind of scowled and said, 'Two-eighty won't do you a damn bit of good.' That really got me hot. I couldn't even finish my hamburger. I just said, 'Watch and see.'

"Well, I was still hot when I got to the first tee. I sort of took my frustrations out on that first tee shot. I knew I'd hit it good the second it left the club. The ball rolled onto the front edge of the green, and I was able to 2-putt for birdie. That got me going, and I shot 65, which, at the time, was the lowest final round in U.S. Open history. That put me at 280, which was good enough to win.

"I hit a lot of good shots that week, but that tee shot at 1 in the final round was a pretty good one under the circumstances."

The 1st hole on a golf course is like the opening scene of a movie, a tone-setter that draws you in without overwhelming you or giving too much away. Most architects agree that the 1st hole should be a challenge but not a beast. Risky options don't usually greet a player right out of the box. Sure, a fairway might run at an odd angle, bringing a plethora of club selections into play, but it's not common for the 1st hole to present a player with a clear-cut, risk-reward decision.

That's what makes the 1st hole at Cherry Hills Country Club unique, and the ideal hole to begin the *Ultimate Eighteen.* It is one of the most picturesque opening holes in the game, offering a downhill vista of a

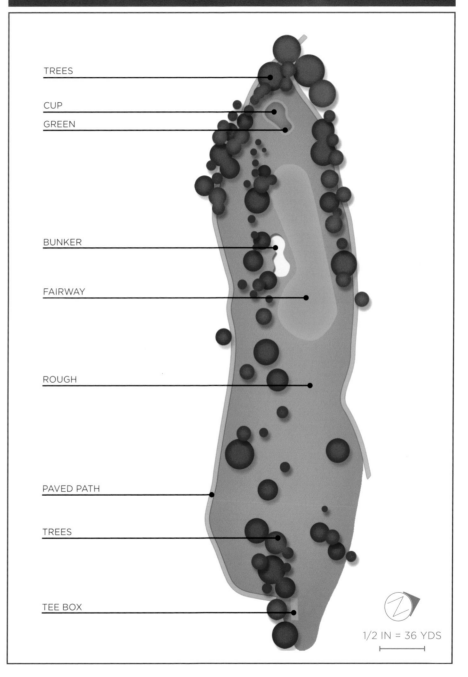

CHERRY HILLS COUNTRY CLUB: 1ST HOLE DIAGRAM

TREES

CUP

GREEN

BUNKER

FAIRWAY

ROUGH

PAVED PATH

TREES

TEE BOX

1/2 IN = 36 YDS

OPPOSITE: *An aerial view of the 1st hole.*

landscape that has challenged players since the course first opened in 1922. As LPGA player Jill McGill, who grew up playing Cherry Hills, says, "There's no better way to start a fantastic round of golf."

The USGA chose Cherry Hills as the first site west of Minneapolis to host the U.S. Open in 1938. Since then it has hosted two PGA Championships, the U.S. Amateur, the U.S. Mid-Amateur, the U.S. Senior Open, the U.S. Women's Open, and two more U.S. Opens, including one of the most famous in the tournament's history.

The 1960 U.S. Open was one of the few times the stars aligned and three generations of champions — past, present, and future — collided in an epic battle. Ben Hogan, the great champion from the forties and fifties and the finest ball-striker the game has ever known, started the final round at one-under-par, while Hogan's playing partner, a pudgy amateur from Ohio named Jack Nicklaus, surprised everyone by staying shot-for-shot with the leaders. Nicklaus also stayed one-under through three rounds. Playing ahead of Hogan

---

"I HIT A LOT OF GOOD SHOTS THAT WEEK, BUT THAT TEE SHOT AT 1 IN THE FINAL ROUND WAS A PRETTY GOOD ONE UNDER THE CIRCUMSTANCES."

—ARNOLD PALMER

---

and Nicklaus, reigning Masters champion Arnold Palmer started the final round seven shots out of the lead. Even though the 1st hole played over 300 yards, the thin Denver air allowed players to fly the ball much farther than they could at sea level, which made the 1st green reachable with a mighty tee shot. Trees blocked the green from a direct approach, with a creek coming into play just to the right as well. Palmer, true to his go-for-broke style, had tried to drive the 1st green every round. Through three rounds, he hadn't done it, and had played the hole 3-over par. But in the final round, Palmer hit what would later be called "the shot heard 'round the world": He drove the first green and made birdie.

Nicklaus and Hogan resisted Palmer's charge until late in the day — and had Hogan not made a late bogey and Nicklaus failed to convert some late putts, the two men might have tied Palmer for a forced playoff. With such contention between the players after Palmer's masterful shot, the 1960 U.S. Open is considered one of the most historic tournaments in the game.

Palmer changed golf forever, and that opening tee shot at Cherry Hills went a long way toward solidifying his legend. Three-time major winner Phil Mickelson also broke onto the scene at Cherry Hills, winning the 1990 U.S. Amateur. And who can forget the dramatic final round of the 2005 U.S. Women's Open? Birdie Kim was tied for the lead with seventeen-year-old amateur Morgan Pressel on the 18th hole when she landed in the sand. Commentator Johnny Miller said, "She has to be careful not to leave this in the bunker, but if she gets it out, she'll be fortunate to keep it on the green." Nevertheless, with Pressel standing in the middle of the 18th fairway, Kim holed an impossible sand shot at the green. Her ball landed fifteen feet short of the hole, hit the flagstick, and fell in for the most improbable birdie in Open history.

But it is Palmer whose legend continues to live at Cherry Hills. Nowhere is his legacy more evident than on the 1st tee, where a plaque proclaims: "Palmer Drove This Green in Final Round."

OPPOSITE: *Cherry Hills Country Club during the U.S. Open, 1960.*

COURSE 3 AT MEDINAH COUNTRY CLUB
2nd Hole

HALE IRWIN

A three-time U.S. Open winner and member of the Hall of Fame, Hale Irwin has eighty-two professional wins on his resume, and is considered one of the grittiest competitors who ever played. He won twenty times on the PGA Tour, putting him in the top tier of all time. But that record pales in comparison to the success that followed. After turning fifty in 1995, Irwin won forty-five times on the Champions Tour, more than any other senior player in history. Today, he designs world-famous courses and continues to compete.

"The 2nd hole at Medinah [in Chicago] is a great, great hole, and a very scary hole, coming as early as it does in the round. I mean, you're coming almost straight out of the box, and suddenly you're faced with this difficult shot of almost 200 yards over water with bunkers back and right and water in the front and on the left. Then the green slopes from back to front so that it makes it very difficult to get the ball up and down if you miss the green. So, if you thought the 1st hole out there was benign, you'd better suck it up for number two. That's a hole that gets your attention very quickly.

"With that green having such a big slope, as most of those greens do at Medinah, any pin location is very difficult. If the pin is on the front and you are short, you're in the water. If you play long you have a very difficult chip or putt down that hill. That sounds pretty tough to me. Of course, I can say that with a smile now because I don't have to play it anymore.

"One of the subtle things that make it so difficult is the fact that you're coming from a relatively secluded teeing area tucked away in a cove with trees, and you're playing out to an open area surrounded by water where the winds can be fickle. Chicago isn't called the Windy City for nothing. It blows

"ANY ARCHITECT WORTH HIS SALT CAN TAKE A GREAT SITE AND DESIGN SOME OF THE BEST HOLES YOU'VE EVER SEEN, BECAUSE HE JUST HAS TO GET OUT OF THE WAY OF MOTHER NATURE. TODAY, WE HAVE TO MANUFACTURE A LOT OF THE THINGS THAT CLASSIC OLD DESIGNERS WERE GIVEN WITH THE LAND."

—HALE IRWIN

there, for sure. So, when you're sitting back on that tee, surrounded by trees, there is a lot of anxiety, because you're not exactly sure what the wind is doing or how hard it's doing it.

"The tendency for most players is to take a little more club, but when you do that, you tend to miss the shot long. Then you've got a very difficult pitch back down the hill toward the water. It's a great hole and the kind of hole you don't find being built much anymore, in part because Medinah was built as a golf club. Today's clubs are built as suburban developments. Back in the twenties when architects were building clubs like Medinah, they could maximize the use of the land and water and other features.

"There is lot to be said for the accommodating aspect of today's game in terms of design, but it certainly takes away from some of the things that made

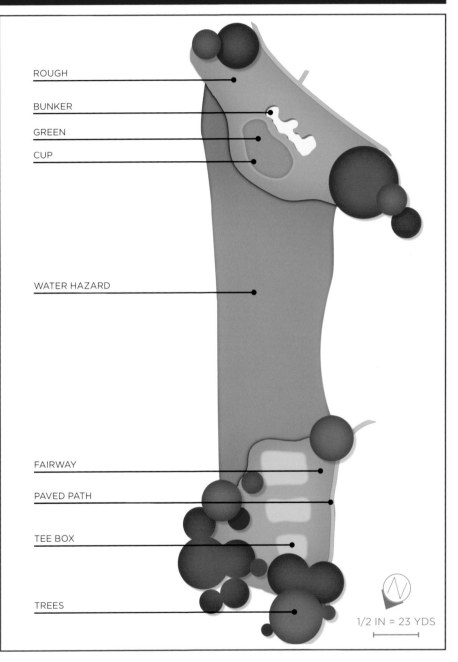

COURSE 3 AT MEDINAH COUNTRY CLUB:
2ND HOLE DIAGRAM

ROUGH

BUNKER

GREEN

CUP

WATER HAZARD

FAIRWAY

PAVED PATH

TEE BOX

TREES

1/2 IN = 23 YDS

OPPOSITE: *The 2nd hole on Course 3 at the Medinah Country Club, host of the 2006 PGA Championship. July 6, 2005.*

19

those old courses what they are. Those old architects went out and found those sites. Any architect worth his salt can take a great site and design some of the best holes you've ever seen, because he just has to get out of the way of Mother Nature. Today, we have to manufacture a lot of the things that classic old designers were given with the land. Members today would be screaming about a hole like number two at Medinah, yelling that it's too tough, or that there aren't enough tees, or the green is too severe, or there's no bailout area. Yet everyone acknowledges that number two is a great hole.

"I just made pars there, and I'm glad. That's a super-hard hole."

In the 1920s, a group of Chicago-area Shriners set out to build the best recreational facility in America. The result was Medinah Country Club. The Tom Bendelow–designed course was recognized instantly as a classic, the kind of course that would challenge the world's greatest golfers for generations to come. With rolling terrain and a mixture of wooded and open holes, Chicago's famous wind made Medinah unpredictable as balls were blown long, short, left, and right. It quickly became a regular venue for some of the nation's premier competitions. Harry "Lighthorse" Cooper won three professional events at Medinah in the early 1930s, and in 1937, Gene Sarazen beat the best players in the game to win the Chicago Open. Two years later, Byron Nelson won the Western Open at Medinah, which was considered a "major" at the time, and in 1946, Nelson won the Chicago Victory Challenge at the club.

In more recent times, the course has hosted three U.S. Opens, a U.S. Senior Open, two PGA Championships, and the 2012 Ryder Cup. Gary Player won a senior major title there, and in 1990, Hale Irwin shot a tournament-low 67 in the final round of the U.S. Open to tie Mike Donald and force a playoff. When he

OPPOSITE: *The pin on the 2nd hole, viewed from the other side of the water hazard.*

holed his final putt to tie the lead, Irwin was so overjoyed that he ran along the edge of the gallery giving high fives to the cheering spectators. On the last day of the tournament, Irwin prevailed in a playoff that took nineteen holes to be decided. He became the oldest winner of the U.S. Open at age forty-five — with five pars on the treacherous 2nd hole, a feat he continues to hold up with great pride.

The two PGA Championships played there in 1999 and 2006 were both won by Tiger Woods. In Tiger's first win, the par-3 2nd hole played a pivotal role. Mike Weir, looking for his first major title, struggled early. On the 2nd hole, he missed the green right, leaving himself a risky pitch shot toward the water. When

"TODAY'S CLUBS ARE BUILT AS SUBURBAN DEVELOPMENTS. BACK IN THE TWENTIES WHEN ARCHITECTS WERE BUILDING CLUBS LIKE MEDINAH, THEY COULD MAXIMIZE THE USE OF THE LAND AND WATER AND OTHER FEATURES."

—HALE IRWIN

he failed to get up and down, Tiger took the lead and never looked back. "You had to feel for Mike," Tiger said at the time. "It just wasn't his day."

Weir hasn't been the only player to fall victim to the perilous par 3. The hole is as close to an island green as you'll find at Medinah, surrounded almost entirely by Lake Kadijah. Only the back right is dry, but that area is guarded by deep bunkers. Tiger managed to play the hole in even par in his two majors. Irwin did the same, and both breathed a sigh of relief when they walked off that green and headed to the 3rd tee.

428 YARDS § PAR 4

OAKMONT COUNTRY CLUB
— *3rd Hole* —

LARRY NELSON

Oakmont in suburban Pittsburgh is considered by most professionals to be the most difficult championship course in America, and its famous "Church Pews" bunker, the 102-yard-long hazard with twelve strips of turf aligned like church pews, is one of the most iconic images in the game. One champion who cracked Oakmont's code was Larry Nelson — he shot a final-round 65 in the 1983 U.S. Open to win over Tom Watson. It was the second of Nelson's three major championship titles, a record that would earn him a spot in the World Golf Hall of Fame. Larry Nelson is always referred to as a quiet, thoughtful man. He is certainly both, but he's also the only modern major champion who did not take up the game of golf until the age of twenty-one. After serving in a combat infantry unit in Vietnam, he taught himself the game by reading Ben Hogan's book *Five Lessons: The Fundamentals of Golf*, and qualified for the PGA Tour only six years after swinging a club for the first time. He went on to capture forty wins as a professional.

"The 3rd hole is a fantastic par 4, definitely one of the best anywhere, but Oakmont is full of those. There isn't a letup anywhere on that course. After two tough opening holes, you see the Church Pews bunker for the first time from the 3rd tee. It has always been intimidating.

"Even though your eye is drawn in that direction, you know you don't want to hit it in there. The problem is, if you let it intimidate you too much, and you bail out too far to the right, you've left yourself with nothing for your approach. There are bunkers down the right side, and the rough is unplayable. From the tee, you're much better off down the left side as close to the Church Pews

OAKMONT COUNTRY CLUB: 3RD HOLE DIAGRAM

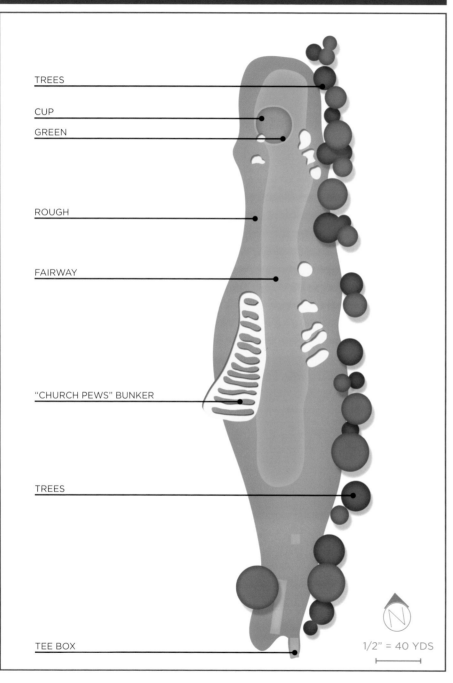

TREES

CUP

GREEN

ROUGH

FAIRWAY

"CHURCH PEWS" BUNKER

TREES

TEE BOX

1/2" = 40 YDS

bunkers as possible to leave you with an easier approach. If you hit it in the right rough, you're pretty much done.

"I've been fortunate in that I don't think I've ever hit it in the Church Pews bunker because I always picked a line down the left center and cut my tee shot so that if I did miss, I was going to miss right. The second problem is that the fairway slopes from left to right and the green is elevated, which means that even if you aren't concerned about the tee shot, the second shot is always going to be tough. The green also slopes left to right, making it very difficult to get the ball close to the hole.

"The most aggressive play is to challenge the Church Pews bunker and leave yourself an easier approach, but if you miss it a little, you're in there and you've got nothing. Or if you bail out too far to the right, you've also got an

> "THE MOST AGGRESSIVE PLAY IS TO CHALLENGE THE CHURCH PEWS BUNKER AND LEAVE YOURSELF AN EASIER APPROACH, BUT IF YOU MISS IT A LITTLE, YOU'RE IN THERE AND YOU'VE GOT NOTHING."
>
> —LARRY NELSON

almost impossible approach. Fortunately, the hole has set up well for me, and I've been able to get through there without any disasters.

"As for Oakmont overall, they've had so many championships there, and the place has so much history it would be hard to deny that it's one of the most talked-about courses in the world. As a fantastic competitive test and one of the great courses of all time, Oakmont is it."

OPPOSITE: *From left to right: Ross Somerville, L. Upson, Robert G. Morrison, and Henry C. Fownes at Oakmont on August 28, 1925.*

Founded and designed by the great amateur player Henry C. Fownes near his Pittsburgh home, Oakmont Country Club opened in 1904 as one of the grandest and most challenging courses in America. It was Fownes's only design, his baby, and he and his sons remained a part of the club for the rest

> "I'VE BEEN FORTUNATE IN THAT I DON'T THINK I'VE EVER HIT IT IN THE CHURCH PEWS BUNKER BECAUSE I ALWAYS PICKED A LINE DOWN THE LEFT CENTER AND CUT MY TEE SHOT SO THAT IF I DID MISS, I WAS GOING TO MISS RIGHT."
>
> —LARRY NELSON

of their lives. It is somewhat unusual that a course designed by an amateur architect, a man who had never drawn a golf hole before and would never draw one again after Oakmont, could create such a timeless masterpiece, a course long recognized as one of the most difficult in the world.

Fownes once said, "A shot poorly played should be a shot irrevocably lost." That attitude is evident on every shot at Oakmont. Long and tight with greens that slope away from the player and 210 bunkers that gobble balls like gremlins, Oakmont continues to confound the greatest players in the world. Before the 2007 U.S. Open, Tiger Woods said, "If you're a 10-handicapper, there is no way you're breaking 100 out there; if you played all out on every shot, there's no way."

The most famous feature on the course is the Church Pews bunker located between the 3rd and 4th hole: It sits ready to catch any leftward shot from either tee. Originally comprising eight separate bunkers, Fownes

redesigned the area in the early 1920s so that it became one expansive bunker with twelve three-foot-high strips of turf lined up like church pews with only four to six yards of sand between them. It is a visually stunning hazard that quickens the pulse and sets the pace for the rest of the round.

Oakmont isn't all torture, though. Johnny Miller set a U.S. Open record when he shot a final-round 63 in 1974 to charge from behind and win. "It's like I'm on the state monument or something when I go around the course," Miller said. "People embrace me and there's a bit of history, and I'm sort of a part of it. It's really a cool feeling out there. I'm out there with different players and they go, 'How the heck did you shoot 63?'"

No one has matched Miller's number, even though Oakmont has hosted more major championships than any other course in North America — eight U.S. Opens, five U.S. Amateurs, three PGA Championships, and two U.S. Women's Opens — with more to come. The list of champions who've won there includes Bobby Jones, Gene Sarazen, Tommy Armour, Ben Hogan, Sam Snead, Patty Sheehan, Ernie Els, and, of course, Jack Nicklaus in a playoff with Arnold Palmer in 1962.

Tied after seventy-two holes, Jack and Arnie squared off in the first of what would become many memorable duels, although this one was all but over before it got underway. Palmer sealed his fate when he bogeyed Oakmont's famous 3rd. Meanwhile, Nicklaus went on something of a tear. By the time Nicklaus rolled in a birdie putt at the 6th, he had a four-shot lead and went on to win his first Open. Palmer said later, "The conventional view is that Oakmont was an Open I should have won because I was the better player at the time. Well, 'should have' and 'did' may be neighbors, but they don't always get along."

OPPOSITE: *Peter Hanson of Sweden hits a shot from the Church Pews bunker during the second round of the 107th U.S. Open at Oakmont Country Club, June 15, 2007.*

BETHPAGE BLACK COURSE
4th Hole

LUCAS GLOVER

A two-time All-American at Clemson University and three-time South Carolina State Amateur Champion, Greenville native Lucas Glover began his professional career in 2002. In 2005, he broke through on the PGA Tour, holing out from the sand on the final hole to win the FUNAI Classic at Disney World. A year later he had nine top-ten finishes, which placed him among the elite top-thirty money winners for the second year in a row. Still, the young pro was not fully appreciated until 2009, when he stared down former world number-one David Duval and world number-two Phil Mickelson to win the U.S. Open at Bethpage Black in Long Island, New York.

"[Number 4 at Bethpage Black] is a great, long par 5 and a good risk/reward hole, a hole you can reach in two and make a birdie on as long as you drive it in the fairway. You have to hit it pretty long out there, but more important than that, you have to be in the fairway. If you're in the rough, you have a terrible time laying up, because there's a large cross bunker that's right where you want to hit it from the rough. If you hit it to the right off the tee, the angle is terrible for a layup, because you want to [land the ball near] the right side of the green. If you're too far to the left off the tee, you probably can't hit it far enough for a decent layup because of the bunkers.

"If you're in the fairway, you're thinking birdie, because you can hit that green with a 5-wood or a long iron, or if you're too far back and can't get it to the green, you lay up to the right and try to get it up and down.

"The green is pretty easy: a straightforward, back-to-front green. But you don't really need much movement on the green on a hole like that. What you want to do is leave it somewhere below the hole so you've got a pretty straightforward putt.

"You have to hit it pretty long out there, but more important than that, you have to be in the fairway. If you're in the rough, you have a terrible time laying up, because there's a large cross bunker that's right where you want to hit it from the rough."

—Lucas Glover

"Because it comes so early in the round, the hole gets overlooked a lot, but it's a great hole and a great opportunity to make a move if you hit it well. But you can certainly struggle there if you don't execute.

"[The 4th] was definitely playing as long as it could on Sunday of the Open — almost all the holes were. With how the wind was blowing, they were all tough. I drove it probably the best I've ever driven it in the first three rounds [of the U.S. Open] there. Not so much the last round. I think nerves played a role in that. But, I was more patient and my attitude was better. When something bad happened, I let it go. I double-bogeyed the 1st hole that week, and didn't slam a club, didn't do anything. I just walked over to the 2nd tee and said: 'Hey, it's the U.S. Open; it's going to be a long week.' I wouldn't have done that a couple years before."

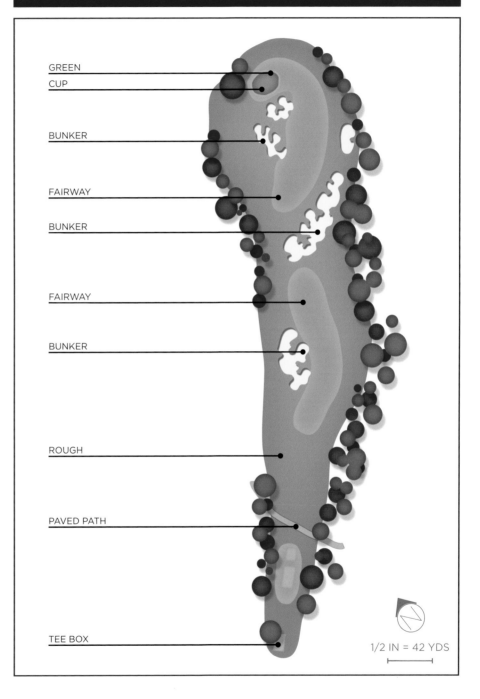

BETHPAGE BLACK COURSE: 4TH HOLE DIAGRAM

GREEN
CUP
BUNKER
FAIRWAY
BUNKER
FAIRWAY
BUNKER
ROUGH
PAVED PATH
TEE BOX

1/2 IN = 42 YDS

OPPOSITE: *An aerial view of the 4th hole at Bethpage Black Course on Long Island, New York. May 30, 2009.*

The largest state-run golf complex in the country, the five courses of the Bethpage State Park meander through wooded Long Island land where three Native American tribes of the Algonquin Nation hunted and farmed

---

"I MUST CONFESS THAT I WAS A TRIFLE SCARED MYSELF WHEN I LOOKED BACK AND REGARDED THE HAZARDOUS ROUTE THAT MUST BE TAKEN BY A STINGING SECOND SHOT TO GET INTO POSITION TO ATTACK THE GREEN."

—A. W. TILLINGHAST, COURSE ARCHITECT

---

for three centuries. When you turn from the 3rd green to the 4th tee at the Black Course, you can sense how rugged and unforgiving the land must have been in 1695 when Englishman Thomas Powell bought the property from the local Native Americans for 140 British pounds. Powell named the area for a quote from the Gospel of St. Matthew 21:1, which says, "When they drew nigh unto Jerusalem and were come to Beth'phage, unto the Mount of Olives."

In 1930, as the Great Depression celebrated its first birthday, the Bethpage State Park Authority was created by State Parks Commissioner Robert Moses. Under the supervision of the legendary golf architect A. W. Tillinghast, the genius behind Winged Foot, Quaker Ridge, Baltusrol, and Ridgewood, construction began on three courses as a Federal Works Administration project that employed 1,800 men. As its centerpiece, the

commission asked Tillinghast to build one course that "might compare with Pine Valley as a great test." Six years later, the Black Course opened with great fanfare.

Long, hilly, wooded, and strewn with bunkers, "the Black," as it's commonly known, has a warning sign on the 1st tee: "The Black Course is an extremely difficult course which we recommend only for highly skilled golfers." The most highly skilled players in the world played it for the first time in 2002 when the U.S. Open came to Bethpage Black. Tiger Woods held off a charging Phil Mickelson to win his second U.S. Open in three years that June. Seven years later, Mickelson seemed poised to redeem himself by winning the 2009 Open at the Black. This time, his efforts were thwarted by Lucas Glover, who shot a final-round 73 to win.

While Glover is a voracious reader, often devouring five books a week, he admits he had not read or heard the comment Tillinghast made about the par-5 4th hole, which he called "one of the finest in the United States." Tillinghast went on to say, "It should prove one of the most exacting 3-shotters I know of anywhere. In locating and designing the green, which can only be gained by a most precise approach from the right, I must confess that I was a trifle scared myself when I looked back and regarded the hazardous route that must be taken by a stinging second shot to get into position to attack the green."

Even though it is not necessarily a "3-shotter," with today's equipment allowing some of the best players in the game to reach the green in two, the hole continues to be as treacherous as any in the game. Sergio Garcia, a Spanish pro who's spent much of his career in the top ten of the World Golf Rankings, called it "a good birdie opportunity, but you have to hit a good tee shot." It is also a hole that can sneak up on a player, especially given how early it comes in the round.

OPPOSITE: *The par-5 4th hole on the Black Course.*

PINEHURST No. 2
5th Hole

MICHAEL CAMPBELL

Other tour players affectionately refer to Michael Campbell as a "grinder," the kind of player who squeezes everything he can out of his game. He isn't an especially long hitter, and he doesn't have a world-class short game. But he's a worker, and when his iron play is on, nobody hits the ball closer to the hole. Lots of players have length, and even more have great touch and marvelous imaginations, but what separates the line of pros on the driving ranges from those with major championship trophies is the relentlessness, the grit found in players like Michael Campbell. That grit led Campbell to fifteen professional wins, including the Irish Open title, the German Masters championship, and the European Open title. But nothing topped his performance in Pinehurst, North Carolina, in 2005. Campbell took on Tiger Woods in a final-round duel that ended with with the native New Zealander, who is also the only player of Maori descent on the pro tour, winning the U.S. Open.

"The 5th hole at Pinehurst No. 2 is a beast, one of the toughest holes on tour, really. It wasn't very kind to me during the 2005 U.S. Open. In four rounds, I scored a par, two bogeys, and then made a par on the last day when I really needed it. It's a tough, tough par 4, and the way it looks, it's tough to gauge.

"It starts out as a real gentle right-to-left dogleg. Even if you hit a perfect tee shot, you still have a long second shot to a tabletop green that runs away in every direction like all the greens at Pinehurst. Only that tabletop has a few wrinkles. What makes the approach so difficult is that you have a strong

PINEHURST NO. 2: 5TH HOLE DIAGRAM

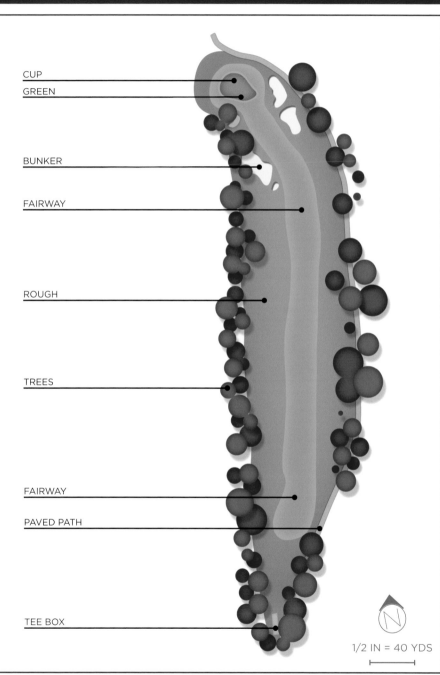

CUP
GREEN
BUNKER
FAIRWAY
ROUGH
TREES
FAIRWAY
PAVED PATH
TEE BOX

1/2 IN = 40 YDS

OPPOSITE: *Bunkers near the green on the 5th hole at Pinehurst No. 2.*

flight of the ball coming in, because it's a longer shot. Those greens are not receptive to any sort of strong incoming ball flight.

"Hitting for the middle of the green is always a great shot, but that's going to leave you a 20- to 30-foot putt on a green that falls away and has a number of ridges throughout. The problem, as is the case with a lot of holes at Pinehurst, is that if you shoot at the pins you'll be 100 percent off the green, 30 or 40 yards away. The greens are crested with roll-offs in every direction. That's one of the reasons the course has held up so well over the years, in my opinion. The greens are so difficult. They are all small, fast, and hard.

"They haven't lengthened the course, so it just proves that you don't have to make a golf course long to make it a great golf course. And you don't have to hit the ball a long way to play a great golf course well. Every hole at Pinehurst is a challenge, and the 5th is one of the best. Look what happened to Tiger. He took double bogey on the 1st hole, and then Retief Goosen took double on the 2nd. Every single hole out there is a new challenge, some turning left, some turning right, some short, some long. You have some incredibly long 4's out there, and some reachable par 5's, which is unusual in a national championship. It's a great blend of holes, a great mix, all of them unique in the challenges they present. The 5th is definitely one of the most challenging."

For the better part of a century, Pinehurst was the world's largest golf resort, with its premier course, No. 2, considered Donald Ross's masterpiece. Ross lived in Pinehurst for more than two decades before his death in 1948, and throughout that time he tinkered with No. 2 until he got it exactly right. His famous greens bulge up from the ground like Native American burial mounds, which makes them beautiful but incredibly hard to hit, hold, and putt.

Of the 413 courses Ross designed in his distinguished career, none is more revered. And no hole typifies the Ross philosophy like the daunting par-4 5th. A great tee shot down the right center still leaves you with a 170- to 200-yard approach to one of Ross's signature crowned greens. As Hall of Famer and broadcaster Johnny Miller said, "The effective hitting area for your approach shot is, basically, nothing. With the greens hard and fast the way the USGA wants them for the [U.S.] Open, you've got about five square feet to hit it in, or it's going to run off into one of Ross's famous chipping areas, where you've got multiple options — you can pitch it, bump and run it with a middle or long iron or even a hybrid or fairway metal, or you can putt it — but none of those options are very appealing. Sometimes you get in there and you say, 'Wow, I hit an awfully good shot to end up with nothing.'" Former number-one ranked pro David Duval summed it up when he said that playing the approach was like "trying to get an 8-iron shot to stop on a pitcher's mound."

That's how Tiger Woods must have felt as he walked away from Pinehurst on two occasions. In 1999, the first time the U.S. Open was held at the venerable North Carolina course, Tiger entered the final round two shots off the lead held by Payne Stewart, and one shot behind Phil Mickelson. Tiger got off to a fast start with a birdie at the 1st hole to draw even with Mickelson and within a shot of Stewart. But Tiger made bogey at the 5th after missing the green and failing to get up and down. He finished the tournament tied for third with Vijay Singh, one shot behind Mickelson and two behind the winner, Stewart.

That U.S. Open turned out to be Stewart's last victory. Four months later, in October of 1999, Stewart was killed in a plane crash. A bronze statue of him sinking the winning putt now stands behind the 18th green at Pinehurst No. 2.

The U.S. Open returned to Pinehurst in 2005, and again Tiger was in contention, although he was far enough back when the final round began that few gave him much of a chance. Defending U.S. Open champion Retief Goosen had a three-shot lead over Olin Browne and Jason Gore in the final, the kind of lead no one expected the normally unflappable Goosen to squander. But squander it he did. A double bogey at the 2nd hole opened the door for Woods and New Zealand's Michael Campbell. Then the 5th claimed another victim: Goosen missed the fairway, which made it virtually impossible for him to reach the green. When he walked off the par 4 with a bogey, his advantage was gone. Campbell, who continued to hit fairways and greens, had the lead.

"YOU'VE GOT ABOUT FIVE SQUARE FEET TO HIT IT IN, OR IT'S GOING TO RUN OFF INTO ONE OF ROSS'S FAMOUS CHIPPING AREAS, WHERE YOU'VE GOT MULTIPLE OPTIONS — YOU CAN PITCH IT, BUMP AND RUN IT WITH A MIDDLE OR LONG IRON OR EVEN A HYBRID OR FAIRWAY METAL, OR YOU CAN PUTT IT — BUT NONE OF THOSE OPTIONS ARE VERY APPEALING."

—JOHNNY MILLER, HALL OF FAMER

The U.S. Open became a showdown between Woods and Campbell, the former being the best player in the game and the latter a dark horse. Given that Campbell hadn't finished in the top ten of a major in ten years, everybody assumed Woods would win. But Campbell never faltered. He made par after par on the holes following the 5th, and stretched his lead to two shots on the back nine, which is where it remained. Tiger made a couple of late bogeys, and Campbell cruised in with an even-par final round for his first major championship title.

OPPOSITE: *Sunset on the 5th green at Pinehurst No. 2, venue for the 2005 U.S. Open, on May 20, 2004.*

430 YARDS § PAR 4

COMPOSITE COURSE AT ROYAL MELBOURNE GOLF CLUB
6th Hole

DAVID GRAHAM

Nobody knows Royal Melbourne in Melbourne, Australia, like David Graham. Winner of thirty-eight professional titles including the PGA Championship and the U.S. Open, the Windsor native is the only Australian to win two different major championships, and one of only two players in history to have won championships on six different continents (the other is South African Gary Player). Graham is also known for having an opinion on everything from politics to science to golf course architecture. That heart-on-his-sleeve brashness bubbled into controversy at the 1996 International Presidents Cup. He had captained the inaugural event in 1994, but as a result of Graham openly speaking his mind, Greg Norman led a mutiny within the team that prevented Graham from following up on his previous triumph. Graham was tough on his team, calling out players he did not think entered the event with the right amount of emotion, a trait that Norman and others found off-putting. But Graham remains outspoken, even though he no longer competes.

"Six at Royal Melbourne is a fantastic par 4, a long dogleg right up a hill with an elevated green that is very, very tough. It's a wonderful test and a testament to the type of architecture that was prevalent back in the 1930s. It's a little bit downhill from the tee, and a really classic design in that you can bite off as much of the dogleg as you feel confident with your drive. If you drive the ball toward the corner of the dogleg you have to negotiate some very craggy bunkers, typical of Royal Melbourne, but if you hit it beyond them and keep it in the fairway you will have a shorter approach. Or you can play to the left from the tee

into a fairly generous landing area, which would be considered safe, but that will leave you a much longer second shot to an elevated green.

"The green is extremely sloped. At today's speeds, it's imperative that your second shot stay on the lower portion of the hole, so you can be putting uphill. If you miss it long, you have a very difficult downhill putt or chip, and if you miss it left or right, you're negotiating an incredibly hard breaking pitch shot. When you think about the technology that was available to architects at the time, the severity of the slopes on those greens makes sense. With today's technology and the speeds we can get on greens today, you would be hammered if you built greens like that now. And yet everyone universally views Royal Melbourne as a fantastic course. It just goes to show how inconsistent golfers can be when it comes to judging what is good and what's not.

"YOU'RE ON THE TEE THINKING, 'THIS DOESN'T LOOK TOO HARD.' BUT IF YOU APPROACH THE HOLE WITH AN ATTACK MODE, AND HIT IT TOO FAR RIGHT, YOU COULD LOSE THE BALL."

—DAVID GRAHAM

"If you look at the [6th] hole strategically, driving the ball right over the bunkers gets you closer to that green, which means you're hitting a shorter club with more loft and spin for your second shot. It is a wonderfully designed par 4 because it gives you options.

"A lot of Alister MacKenzie holes lull you to sleep because you think you have expansive landing areas for the tee shot. The 6th is one of those. You're on the tee thinking, 'This doesn't look too hard.' But if you approach the hole with an attack mode, and hit it too far right, you could lose the ball. If you pull it too

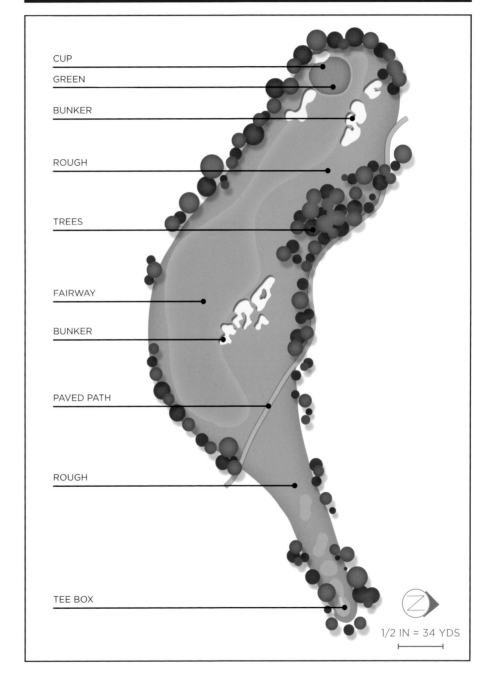

COMPOSITE COURSE AT ROYAL MELBOURNE GOLF CLUB: 6TH HOLE DIAGRAM

CUP
GREEN
BUNKER
ROUGH
TREES
FAIRWAY
BUNKER
PAVED PATH
ROUGH
TEE BOX

1/2 IN = 34 YDS

OPPOSITE: *The 6th hole on the Composite Course at Royal Melbourne Golf Club.*

far left, you could be in the high wispy grass. It's a tee shot that gives you a false sense of security.

"You don't see holes like that much anymore, because designers don't get pieces of properties like the one at Royal Melbourne. The growth of the trees has made it more challenging. Plus, the greens in the early thirties weren't any better than the fairways today, so architects could add a lot of slopes and undulations. You throw all of that into the mix, and you understand the genius behind a design like Royal Melbourne."

A national treasure, Royal Melbourne was established in 1891 as Australia's first golf club, although it was first located closer to the Melbourne city center than the modern course. Alister MacKenzie and his disciples designed the current two golf courses, the West Course and the East Course, and both are consistently ranked among the the top one hundred courses in the world. They opened to great fanfare in 1931. But it is the Composite Course — an adaptation using twelve holes from the West Course and six from the East Course — that has been the site of numerous championships and is consistently ranked as one of the top ten courses in the world. Royal Melbourne has hosted

more Australian Opens than any other course in the country, and was the host club for the Presidents Cup in 1998 and hosts it again in 2011.

Of all the holes on the Composite Course, the 6th is widely regarded as the best par 4 on the continent. Greg Norman called it "one of the greatest par 4's in the world," even though Norman didn't win any of his five Australian Open titles at the famous course. He was on the winning Presidents Cup team that demolished the Americans at Royal Melbourne in 1998, a team that was captained by Australia's other stalwart, Peter Thomson. Thomson, a five-time winner of the British Open, began his career as an assistant pro at Royal Melbourne.

The course is full of great par 4's, but the 6th has it all. An elevated tee shot to a huge fairway gives the player numerous options. The hole doglegs right, but trying to avoid the fairway bunkers only brings deeper and more treacherous green-side bunkers into play. Depending on the wind and the quality of the drive, a player can have anything from a 3-iron to a 9-iron for his second shot to a green that looks like a roller coaster. With a seemingly generous landing area from the tee, but with trade-offs throughout, this hole makes it easy to see the design philosophy that became a trademark of MacKenzie courses like Cypress Point, Pasatiempo, and Augusta National. Even though the designer provided ample space to play, there is a narrowly defined path to follow to make birdies. As is often the case with the greatest holes, the 6th demands that golfers walk a fine line between victory and defeat. That's a challenge no top player can resist.

ABOVE: *A scenic view toward the pin on the 6th hole.* **OPPOSITE:** *The 6th hole of the Composite Course.*

"It keeps you out of your element the whole way."

OAK HILL COUNTRY CLUB
7th Hole

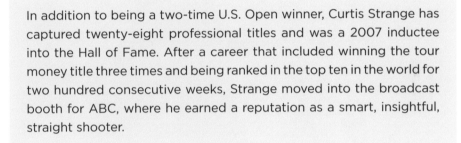

CURTIS STRANGE

In addition to being a two-time U.S. Open winner, Curtis Strange has captured twenty-eight professional titles and was a 2007 inductee into the Hall of Fame. After a career that included winning the tour money title three times and being ranked in the top ten in the world for two hundred consecutive weeks, Strange moved into the broadcast booth for ABC, where he earned a reputation as a smart, insightful, straight shooter.

"Seven at Oak Hill [in Rochester, New York] is a great par 4 on a course that's full of great, tough par 4's. That hole is a little different in that it doesn't look that difficult when you get there, but it keeps you out of your element the whole way. There is a creek that runs down the right side that then crosses the fairway. It's a solid tee shot that keeps you somewhat off balance because it's semi-blind over a little crest. The creek certainly comes into play if you drive it right into the rough. So driving is at a premium. The second shot also keeps you off balance because it's back uphill and the trees are always there, creating this tunnel effect. It's important to pay close attention and not be too intimidated. The approach can be pretty long, so if you choose to play right at the hole from that distance you could be left with a difficult birdie opportunity.

"The green slopes from back to front, so you have to be aware of the pin position. If you get above the hole, you'll have one of the tougher putts of

OAK HILL COUNTRY CLUB: 7TH HOLE DIAGRAM

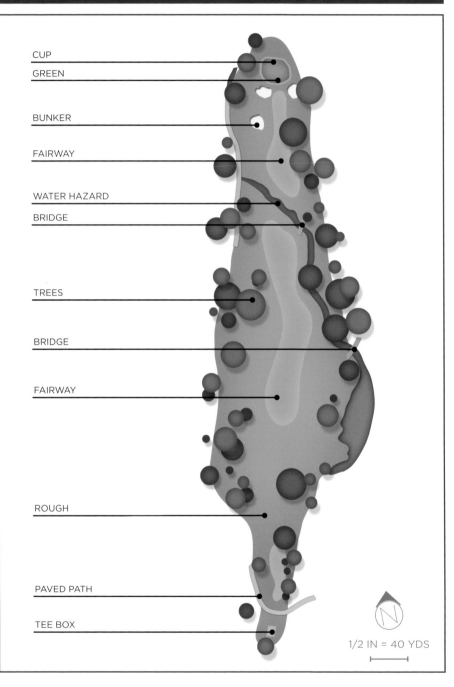

CUP
GREEN
BUNKER
FAIRWAY
WATER HAZARD
BRIDGE
TREES
BRIDGE
FAIRWAY
ROUGH
PAVED PATH
TEE BOX

1/2 IN = 40 YDS

OPPOSITE: *The 7th hole is called "The Creek's Elbow" for the water hazard that runs across it.*

your life. It's a good solid hole, as most of the par 4's at Oak Hill are. I mean, for me, the 6th is an example of a very good, solid U.S. Open par 4. There is nothing tricky about it. The premium is on the tee shot. If you miss the fairway, the creek crossing the fairway and the slope of the green make it very uncomfortable.

"I look at that entire golf course as an example of what architects should do when given a great piece of property. Sure, on a bad piece of property, you have to move some dirt, but I don't understand why today's architects feel the need to move so much dirt around when the greatest golf courses in the world — the ones we continue to put on pedestals and try to emulate — were built with minimal earth moving. Oak Hill is on a fantastic piece of land, and, of course, architects did not move a lot of dirt back then because they really couldn't. The technology wasn't available. You just went with what was there. But the results are great.

"It's unrelenting when you play an Open there. I'm still trying to figure out where the birdie opportunities are. It's a lot of golf course, and 7 is the best example of that."

Prior to playing the 2003 PGA Championship, Tiger Woods called Oak Hill "one of the fairest and toughest major championship courses out there." This was before Tiger hooked tee shots at the 7th into the left rough three of the four days, however. After those unsettling shots, he could never get anything going, while winner Shaun Micheel, who hit a miraculous shot to within an inch of the final hole, parred the 7th on the last two days to retain the lead and capture his first major championship title.

Ernie Els, who played the 7th one-over-par for the week, echoed Woods, calling Oak Hill "the best, fairest, and toughest championship golf course I've ever played in all my years as a tour professional." These were not off-

the-cuff comments. In fact, Woods and Els were repeating sentiments that had been coming from professionals for decades. Sam Snead was singing praises for the Donald Ross masterpiece as early as 1941. "This course is certainly one of the finest I have ever seen, fit for either an Open or a PGA," Snead said.

Called "The Creek's Elbow," the exacting hole is a classic. With a creek that runs diagonally across the fairway from 220 to 260 yards, short hitters must play to the right-center of the fairway, which leaves them with a more difficult approach. Longer hitters can play up the left side, making the second shot much easier. It is a tough par 4 designed by a master, one that has earned the respect of all who have played it.

In 1968, Lee Trevino came on to the scene at Oak Hill, making four pars on the 7th to beat Jack Nicklaus by four shots for the U.S. Open title. He became the first man in the history of the Open to shoot four rounds in the sixties.

History was made again in Rochester in 1980 when Jack Nicklaus won the PGA Championship at Oak Hill by seven shots over Miller Barber. It was Nicklaus's second major of the season and the seventeenth professional major of his career. Since he was already forty years old at the time, many assumed Oak Hill was Nicklaus's last hurrah — an assumption he quashed in 1986 when he won the Masters in what many consider the greatest golf tournament ever played.

Curtis Strange came within a shot of the U.S. Open single-round scoring record when he posted a 64 on Friday at Oak Hill. But it was his final-round consistency, with sixteen pars, one birdie, and one bogey, that is best remembered. One of the holes where Strange ground out a series of pars was the par-4 7th. That round made Strange the first man to win back-to-back

---

"THE GREEN SLOPES FROM BACK TO FRONT, SO YOU HAVE TO BE AWARE OF THE PIN POSITION. IF YOU GET ABOVE THE HOLE, YOU'LL HAVE ONE OF THE TOUGHER PUTTS OF YOUR LIFE."

—CURTIS STRANGE

U.S. Opens since Ben Hogan had done it in 1950 and 1951. "It was emotional last year," Strange said at the 1989 awards ceremony in front of the Oak Hill clubhouse. "This year it's more of a feeling of satisfaction, I guess; a feeling of accomplishment, because to win the Open two years in a row is really something. It's hard to describe the feeling." It remains one of the rarest feats in golf.

ABOVE: *Overlooking the 7th hole at Oak Hill Country Club.* **OPPOSITE:** *A view of the 7th green at Oak Hill.*

ROYAL TROON GOLF CLUB
—— *8th Hole* ——

TOM WEISKOPF

In an era of tough competitors, Tom Weiskopf won only one major despite his famous swing. He finished second in the Masters four times and was runner-up in the 1976 U.S. Open. He did win the U.S. Senior Open before retiring from competition, but his greatest moment was his British Open victory at Royal Troon in Troon, Scotland. Now one of the top golf course architects in the world, Weiskopf has also worked as a television analyst for CBS and ABC. Still considered one of the more cerebral pros who ever played, Weiskopf has fond memories of Royal Troon, particularly the 8th.

"One of my greatest experiences in the game was being a spectator standing in the middle of the 7th fairway at Royal Troon for two consecutive days in 1973 and watching Gene Sarazen play in the 8th hole. Although I couldn't see the green, I could see the flagstick, because the 7th fairway is well below the 8th green. Gene was seventy-one years old at the time, but he had been invited to play as a former champion. On the first day, the first round, I'm standing in the 7th fairway waiting for the green to clear, and I saw Gene make a birdie 2 on the 8th by holing his second shot from the front, right bunker. This is particularly poignant since Gene is recognized as the historical creator of the sand wedge.

"The next day, second round, I'm standing in the same spot and Gene is on the tee again. I see him hole his tee shot for a hole-in-one. He played the

hole in a grand total of three shots for two days, and never used a putter. Now that is as much history as you need on one particular hole. To me that should be equally as famous at Gene's double eagle at Augusta National when he won the Masters. I witnessed something historic, that's for sure.

"As for the 8th itself, most all the holes in the British Isles have names, and that one is the Postage Stamp for good reason. The only other hole I can think of that could legitimately have that name is the 7th at Pebble Beach. When the wind blows, it is certainly a postage stamp green.

"I BELIEVE HOLES LIKE THIS ARE POPULAR — AND WE ALWAYS TALK ABOUT SHORT HOLES LIKE THIS — BECAUSE EVERYBODY HAS A CHANCE ON THEM. A SHORT HOLE LIKE THE 8TH GIVES EVERY PLAYER OF EVERY LEVEL A CHANCE TO PLAY THE HOLE WITHIN THE CONFINES AND CONTEXTS OF HIS OR HER OWN GAME."

—TOM WEISKOPF

Depending on the conditions, the club selection can range from a sand wedge to a 6- or 7-iron. [The green is] well protected, and slightly downhill on the tee shot, probably a ten-foot drop from tee to green. Everything is very visible, including the huge, deep bunker right in front. There is another bunker to the right that is even deeper than the first. Then there is a sliver bunker located in a sand dune on the left that guards the entire left two-thirds of the green. That bunker is elevated slightly above green level, and is just big enough for an angry man and a club. You can get some horrendous lies in there.

"Believe it or not, that left bunker, under difficult conditions, is your bailout, because under no circumstances do you want to be in those deep bunkers on the right. If you get into the bunkers on the right, you cannot see the surface of the green. Then it's a slight kidney-shaped green, very similar in size to the 7th at Pebble. In my opinion, it's the most memorable short hole in championship golf.

"I was very fortunate in that I never missed the green in four rounds, so I was able to walk away with four pars. But it can be, in certain wind conditions, just horrible. It's the first hole where you turn back toward the clubhouse and the sea after playing the first seven holes out. Behind it and to the left is a long-distance view of the sea and well to the left of the biggest dune is the Ailsa Craig. When you play that hole into the wind, you know that you're in for a difficult back nine once you turn back for good toward the clubhouse.

"I believe holes like this are popular — and we always talk about short holes like this — because everybody has a chance on them. A short hole like the 8th gives every player of every level a chance to play the hole within the confines and contexts of his or her own game. A statistic I read twenty-two years ago in a brochure from the National Golf Foundation said that of the 22 million golfers in the United States at that time — and they defined a golfer as anyone who played ten rounds a season — 92 percent of those people do not break 90. Only one-half of one percent break 80 and even less break 70. But all of those players, regardless of what they shoot or how often they play, have a chance to make a birdie or a par on these short holes. It's not easy, but it's possible. They don't have the power off the tee to hit shots like Tiger Woods on the long holes, but when you talk about the great short holes, they say, 'Hey, I have a chance here.' That's why everybody talks about the short holes.

OPPOSITE: *The 8th hole at Royal Troon, known as the "Postage Stamp."*

ROYAL TROON GOLF CLUB: 8TH HOLE DIAGRAM

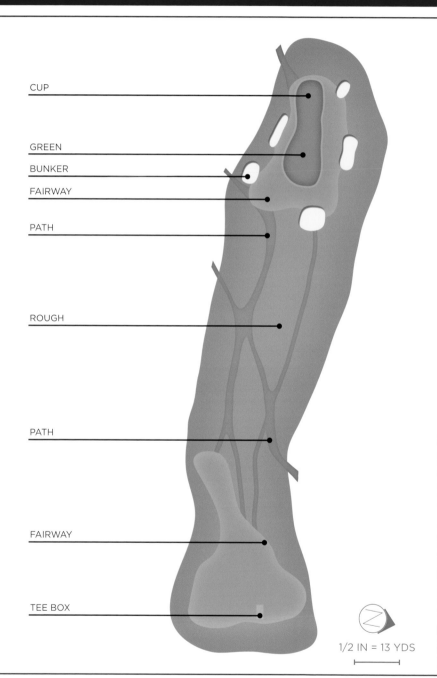

CUP

GREEN

BUNKER

FAIRWAY

PATH

ROUGH

PATH

FAIRWAY

TEE BOX

1/2 IN = 13 YDS

OPPOSITE: *A greenkeeper grooms one of the bunkers at Royal Troon's 8th hole.*

"It also makes the better player nervous because everybody knows that they can make a big number on a hole like this if they aren't precise. Holes like the 8th at Troon define risk/reward. It's a fair challenge, and under certain conditions, holes like this really penalize a marginal shot. It is a hole that can equalize the playing field very quickly."

The shortest hole on all of the courses that host the British Open, the "Postage Stamp," as it is called, is one of the best little holes in the game with a green that is only twenty-five feet wide. Surrounded by bunkers and dunes,

"THERE IS A SLIVER BUNKER LOCATED IN A SAND DUNE ON THE LEFT THAT GUARDS THE ENTIRE LEFT TWO-THIRDS OF THE GREEN. THAT BUNKER IS ELEVATED SLIGHTLY ABOVE GREEN LEVEL, AND IS JUST BIG ENOUGH FOR AN ANGRY MAN AND A CLUB."

—TOM WEISKOPF

the 8th is either a hit-the-green birdie opportunity, or a hole where you can run up a high score. In traditional links style, the first seven holes play out along the shoreline, running the same direction parallel to the coast. The 8th is the first hole that turns back toward the clubhouse, giving the golfer a glimpse of what the wind conditions will be like when the course turns inward for good at the 10th.

In 1923, Walter Hagen lost the British Open by one shot after making a 6 at the 8th in the final round. His tee shot found the deep, treacherous

bunker on the right, and he failed to get out with his first shot from the sand. He finally knocked his ball onto the green, only to take three putts. Bobby Locke and Arnold Palmer won the Open there after successfully negotiating the 8th all four days. Todd Hamilton also survived the 8th in his upset win over Ernie Els in 2004. But at the 1950 Open, German amateur Herman Tissies made a 15 on this short hole, hitting one tee shot, one putt, and *thirteen* bunker shots.

In 1997, Tiger Woods, coming off a record-setting 64 in the third round and looking for a Sunday charge, hit what he thought was a perfect wedge, but found the bunker. From the sand, he hit the parapet and rolled back into the bottom of the bunker. His third shot skidded across the green, and it took him three putts to get down. Later in the day, Colin Montgomerie took a 5 at the Postage Stamp, and fell from contention. Justin Leonard,

who grew up playing in the Texas wind, bunted a pitching wedge to the front edge of the 8th and went on to win his one and only major.

In 1973, the man with what many (including Jack Nicklaus) considered the greatest swing in golf finally broke through and won his first major at Royal Troon. Tom Weiskopf is one of the most talented ball-strikers who ever lived, but a fiery temper and the fact that he played in the era of Nicklaus, Johnny Miller, Lee Trevino, and Tom Watson left him as the game's ultimate bridesmaid. He reached as high as the number two ranking in the world behind Nicklaus nonetheless, proving that finishing second on that list was itself the mark of a champion.

ABOVE: *A view out to the ocean, looking over the "Postage Stamp" hole at Royal Troon.*
OPPOSITE: *The 8th green.*

"It's definitely one of the all-time great par 5's."

510 YARDS § PAR 5

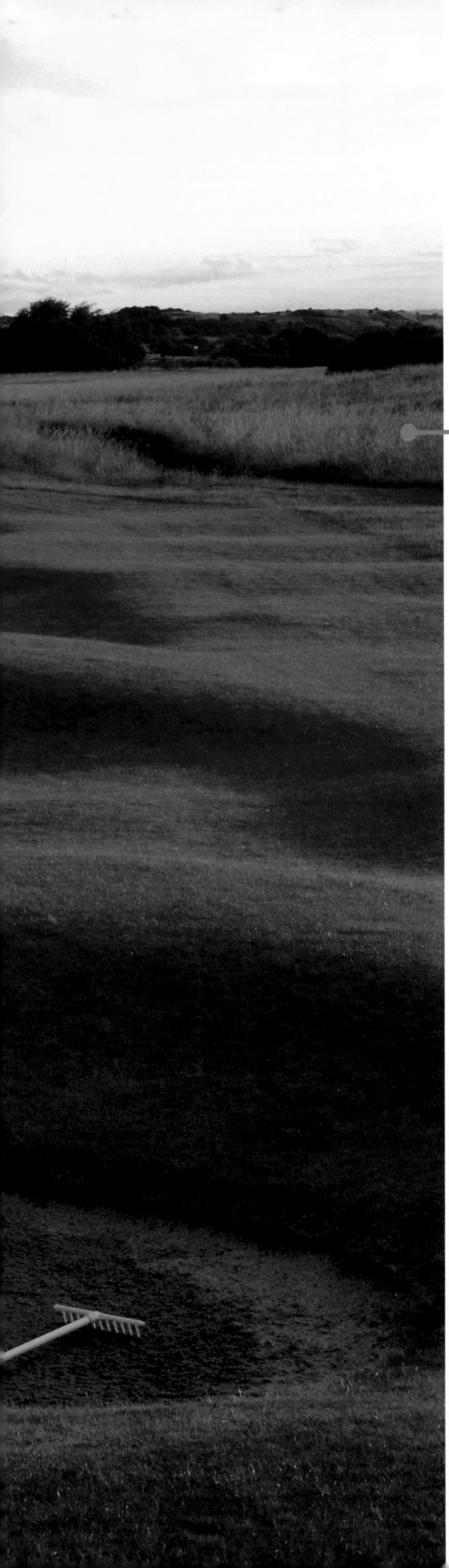

MUIRFIELD

9th Hole

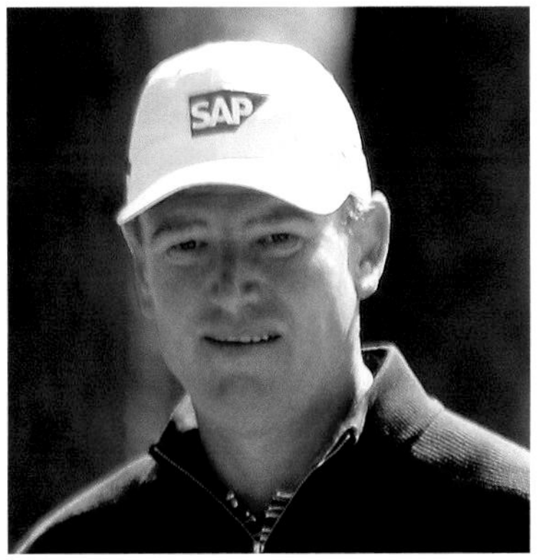

ERNIE ELS

Winner of sixty-four professional titles around the world, including two U.S. Opens in the 1990s, South African player Ernie Els set a record for staying in the top ten of the World Golf Rankings for 750 weeks. In 2002, he finally hoisted the Claret Jug, the trophy he wanted more than any other, at Muirfield in Edinburgh, Scotland, in no small part because he managed to avoid any hiccups at the treacherous 9th.

"It's definitely one of the all-time great par 5's, with a wall and bunkers guarding the left side and a fairway that gets narrower the farther down you go. If you can get it around the first set of bunkers from the tee, you can reach the green fairly easily, although the green is semi-blind. But there is a lot of trouble [to the] right. With today's technology, you can almost get there with two 3-woods, depending on the conditions. Still, it is quite a narrow area. It is definitely one of those holes where, if you hit two good shots, you can make an easy 5, and if you miss by just a fraction, you can make an ugly 7. That, in my opinion, is the mark of a great hole. There is risk, and there is reward, but to be rewarded, you have to get it exactly right.

"You can always play safe and play for your par, or depending on the conditions and how well you are hitting the ball at the time, you can be aggressive and try to make birdie or even eagle. I always thought of it as a birdie hole, and I was fortunate enough to play it 3-under for the week in

MUIRFIELD: 9TH HOLE DIAGRAM

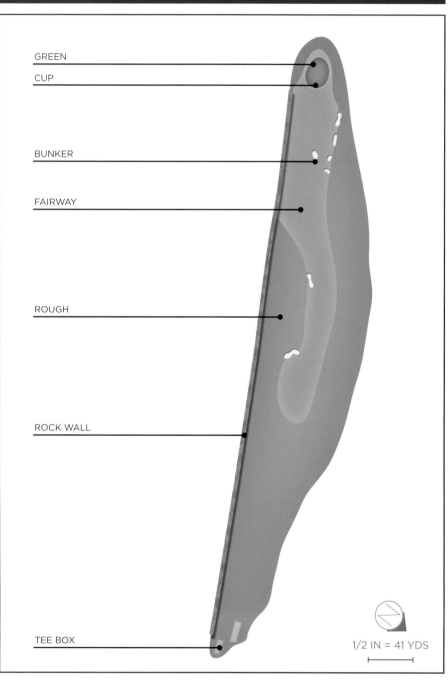

GREEN

CUP

BUNKER

FAIRWAY

ROUGH

ROCK WALL

TEE BOX

1/2 IN = 41 YDS

2002, but that was all set up because I was able to hit the ball in the fairway. That fairway is also very tough to hold, because it tends to push your ball to the right. If you miss the fairway and end up in the rough, you have a difficult layup because of all the bunkers. I was able to thread the tee shot in there, so I was able to hit a low second shot that hit in front of the green and ran, as happens a lot on hard, fast links courses like that.

"Once you're on the green, there isn't much there, but there doesn't need to be much there. Like most of the holes at Muirfield, the green at the 9th is very straightforward — [there are] no gimmicks. I think it's one of the greatest golf courses in the world, full of a lot of very special holes. The 9th is certainly one of those, a great par 5 that has stood the test of time and continues to be as challenging today as it ever was."

Designed by Old Tom Morris in 1891, the links course at Muirfield is, according to Jack Nicklaus, the best in the British Open rotation, and one of the greatest tests of golf in the world. "It's a great test of skill, patience, and a player's ability to execute all types of shots under many different conditions," Nicklaus said. He loved the course so much that, when it came time to build his own masterpiece in his hometown of Dublin, Ohio, he chose to name the place Muirfield Village.

All the holes at Muirfield present the player with numerous options, starting at the 1st, where players can tee off with anything from a 4-iron to a driver, depending on their confidence and how much risk they want to take. That same strategy can be employed on the 2nd, 3rd, and throughout the rest of the course. It is especially evident on the par-5 9th, a relatively short 3-shot hole by modern standards, which can play even shorter with the prevailing wind behind and the fairways brick-hard.

Usually a short, downwind par 5 is something players can't wait to reach, but the 9th at Muirfield is an exception to that rule. In classic Muirfield

OPPOSITE: *The 9th tee at Muirfield in Scotland.*

risk/reward fashion, the longer a player hits it off the tee, the more claustrophobic the hole becomes. The landing area is a generous 50 yards wide at the 250-yard mark, but from there the hole gets progressively narrower. A tee shot of 300 yards must be threaded into a sliver of turf no more than 20 yards

> "IF YOU HIT TWO GOOD SHOTS, YOU CAN MAKE AN EASY 5, AND IF YOU MISS BY JUST A FRACTION, YOU CAN MAKE AN UGLY 7."
>
> —ERNIE ELS

wide with several bunkers guarding both sides of the tightening fairway and a rock wall creeping into play on the left as you approach the green. If your nerves are good, the hole can be a catalyst for great things, as Lee Trevino discovered when he made an eagle there in the final round of the 1972 British Open. That hole propelled Trevino to victory over Jack Nicklaus and Tony Jacklin. The 9th is also the home of heartbreak, as Peter Thomson found out in 1959 when he pulled his second shot over the wall on the left side of the green and missed his chance to become the first man ever to win five British Opens in six years.

In 1992, Nick Faldo arrived at Muirfield in search of his third British Open title. He had won his first Open in 1987 at Muirfield, and his second in 1990 at St. Andrews. The hottest player in the world at the time, Faldo felt great about his game — but a first-round score of 66 left Faldo two shots behind Americans Steve Pate and Raymond Floyd. It wasn't until he reached the 9th tee in the second round that things turned Faldo's way for good.

"I hit my drive down that right-hand side, just out of the fairway," Faldo recalled, "and then I hit an example of what I call one of my 'knuckle-dusters,' a really low-running 3-wood. There's a hump short of the green on the right side and I said to myself, 'Well, if you hit it there it should bounce up near the hole,' so I hit the thing and it barely got ten feet off the ground, and it scooted off [the mound], using the ground to my full advantage. It hit and hopped and ran up there about four feet from the hole. When you can pull shots off like that, it keeps you going." Faldo made eagle to take the lead. From there, he never looked back. He hit fairways and greens throughout the back nine, and marched triumphantly up the final fairway as the winner of his third Open title.

ABOVE: *Ernie Els hits a bunker shot during the final round of the 131st British Open, held at Muirfield, July 21, 2002.* **OPPOSITE:** *The treeless 9th green at Muirfield.*

"It's a hole that tests your ego and your instincts."

RIVIERA COUNTRY CLUB
— *10th Hole* —

AMY ALCOTT

Riviera member and LPGA Hall of Famer Amy Alcott consulted with the members of the elite Los Angeles club in restoring the famous 10th hole to its original condition. A thoughtful tactician of the game, Alcott was an LPGA winner as a teenager and was named Rookie of the Year at age twenty. Among her five major championship titles, she won the Kraft Nabisco Championship three times, and was the U.S. Women's Open champion in 1980 — an amazing season in which Alcott won four times, finished second five times, and was in the top ten in twenty-one out of twenty-eight events she played. The winner of twenty-five LPGA tournaments, Amy remains one of the smartest and most articulate players in the game, a champion with hundreds of friends in the game and millions of fans.

"The 10th at Riviera is one of my favorite holes in the world, and definitely one of the greatest short par-4's anywhere. It's a hole that tests your ego and your instincts. A lot of guys can take driver and even 3-wood and hit the green, but if you miss it a little bit right, you don't have a shot. There is plenty of room to the left, and if you take an iron and lay it up to the left you have a straightforward pitch.

"There is also plenty of room to the right, so it's very tempting to swing away with reckless abandon, but you have to respect the trouble that comes from having such a long but narrow green. If you hit it out to the left, you open up the green, but if you hit it right and miss the green, you have almost no shot.

"There are a lot of holes in golf that are like that — total risk/reward holes. As a player I always appreciated the genius of some of the older designers, and now, as a course designer [myself], I really love the subtlety and strategy that goes into wonderful older holes like the 10th at Riviera. They might need a face-lift, but they never really require an overhaul. It's funny, because I'm talking to a lot of players who are now in the architectural business, and they all go back to the classic old courses when discussing their philosophy. And all of them will, invariably, mention a short hole, especially a short par 4, somewhere in the conversation.

> "IT'S VERY TEMPTING TO SWING AWAY WITH RECKLESS ABANDON, BUT YOU HAVE TO RESPECT THE TROUBLE THAT COMES FROM HAVING SUCH A LONG BUT NARROW GREEN."
>
> —AMY ALCOTT

"Many great golf courses have been taken out of the competitive professional rotation because they are deemed too short. That is not only a shame, it's also wrongheaded. The old Donald Ross, [A. W.] Tillinghast, and George Thomas courses are still some of the greatest tests in the game. Riviera [a Thomas design] proves that. A course doesn't have to be that long to be tough and challenging, just like a hole doesn't have to be long and daunting to be a great test.

"Everybody hits it longer now, so that has to be taken into account, but it's still the short 4's that are very tempting. Those are the holes that people are always talking about. They're the ones that are exciting. Of those, the 10th at Riviera, with its small, tough green, is one of the best in the world."

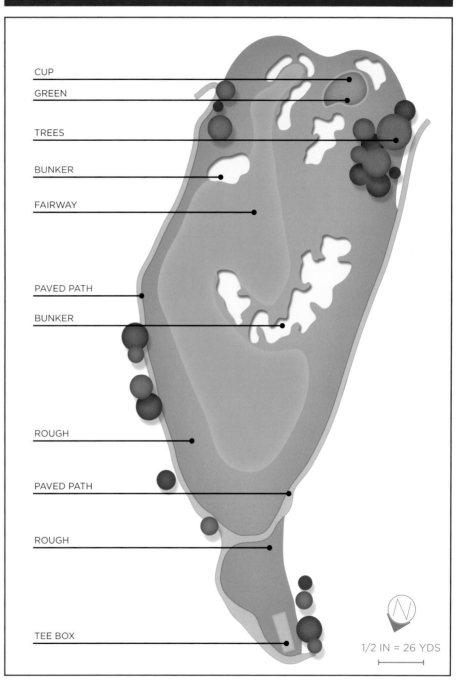

RIVIERA COUNTRY CLUB: 10TH HOLE DIAGRAM

CUP
GREEN
TREES
BUNKER
FAIRWAY
PAVED PATH
BUNKER
ROUGH
PAVED PATH
ROUGH
TEE BOX

1/2 IN = 26 YDS

OPPOSITE: *View of the 10th green at Riviera Country Club.*

A California gem, Riviera Country Club earned its championship credentials not long after it opened in 1927. MacDonald Smith won the Los Angeles Open there in 1928, and since then players like Byron Nelson, Sam Snead, Tom Watson, Johnny Miller, Hal Sutton, Nick Faldo, Ernie Els, Fred Couples, and Phil Mickelson have all won titles at Riviera. Notably absent from that list is Tiger Woods, who set a personal record at Riviera that he would rather forget. In eleven appearances, he failed to win the Los Angeles Open a single time, the most starts he's ever made in an event without logging a win.

On the other hand, Ben Hogan hoisted a number of trophies at Riviera, so many in fact that the place became known as "Hogan's Alley," a nickname thrust onto the course by Hogan's friend Jimmy Demaret after Hogan won the 1947 and 1948 Los Angeles Opens and the 1948 U.S. Open at Riviera, all within a span of eighteen months. Hogan's wins were a model of precision and discipline. For example, in every round Hogan played the short par-4 10th with an iron layup off the tee, and a pitch to the narrow green. As a result he was under par on the hole for his career. The same is true for 1983 PGA Championship winner Hal Sutton, who could have easily driven the 10th, but chose to play safely to the left in capturing his one and only major.

ABOVE: *Bo Van Pelt of the U.S. and Retief Goosen of South Africa approach the 10th green during the final round of the 2007 Nissan Open at the Riviera Country Club.*
OPPOSITE: *A scenic view of the well-protected 10th green during the second round of the Northern Trust Open, February 15, 2008.*

Through all the years, the most talked-about hole on the course remains the 10th. One of the best drivable par 4's in the world, it has been tempting players since Bobby Jones tried to drive the green in 1930. Today, players stand on the tee knowing they only need to fly their tee shot 280 yards to reach the front of the green, but missing the small target brings in all sorts of difficulties. As two-time Masters winner Ben Crenshaw said, "There are so many different, tough shots around the green. For me, it was just too much to take if I hit driver off the tee and it didn't work out. It could get me out of sorts for the rest of the round."

Noted golf course architect Tom Doak said, "Of all the great golf holes in America, the 10th might be the least imposing to the untrained eye. It's certainly the flattest great hole I've seen." And great it is. Jack Nicklaus called it his favorite short par 4 in the world, and Phil Mickelson said, "It's really one of the best short holes in the game."

PGA Champion and Ryder Cup hero Paul Azinger explained why the layup to the left is a smarter play. "Good players will almost always hit shots from outside 100 yards pin high. The misses from that distance are left or right, not distance misses. From inside 100 yards, good players almost always hit the ball on line. The misses from that distance are short or long. So, if you have a long narrow green, you want to be hitting a short shot into it, because you're going to get that shot on line, and if you dial in the right distance, you're pretty close to the hole." With a small landing area for a short pitch, and peril awaiting any shot that misses the target, that precision is paramount on the Riviera's classic 10th.

BALLYBUNION OLD COURSE
— *11th Hole* —

CHRISTY O'CONNOR JR.

Galway's Christy O'Connor Jr. grew up on the southwest links of Ireland. He went on to win the Irish Open and the Senior British Open but is most famous for his heroics for Europe in the 1989 Ryder Cup. Europe led those matches by two points going into the final-round singles at the Belfry outside Birmingham, England. One of the matches the Americans desperately needed to win was that of Fred Couples, who was favored to beat O'Connor. Their match came down to the final green, but O'Connor prevailed, handing Europe what would turn out to be the crucial point in the matches. The two teams tied, but since Europe held the cup, having won the 1987 matches, they retained it thanks to O'Connor's upset victory.

O'Connor can imagine no other venue with more to offer than the 11th at Ballybunion in Ireland. "A jolly," as they would say in pubs from Doolin to Galway, O'Connor is the consummate Irish gentleman golfer, witty and wry, with a lyrical flair for understatement.

"When you talk about quality golf holes, it's impossible to top the 11th at the Ballybunion Old Course. It's a hugely popular and spectacular golf hole, followed and loved closely by Tom Watson and, of course, everyone in Ireland. Part of what makes it so great is the combination of beautiful views with the requirement of challenging golf shots.

"The hole sits on several plateaus. The tee is on one plateau jutting out over the cliffs seventy feet above the beach with the most gorgeous views you can imagine of the sea to your right. I mean, you look out there and your next stop is

Boston. You're looking down from the tee to the second plateau, which is your landing area. You're better off if the tee shot stays on that second level, because it runs out at about 300 yards. Hit it farther than that, and you'll have a terrible downhill lie for your second shot. There are massive dunes on the left-hand side. If you're up there, you might as well head in. There's virtually no escape. Then, blending in the right-hand side is a magnificent beach.

"For your second shot you have to thread the ball through two sand dunes about 30 yards short of the green. You can just see the green through them. If you can thread your second shot through those dunes, man, it's like a tonic; it's wonderful. The green then falls off in every direction into thick rough. If you're lucky enough to make par there, run to the bar. Forget about playing the rest of the golf course. Your day won't get any better.

"It's one of the greatest golf courses in the world and one of the most beautiful in Ireland. I once shot 63 there with a 9 on the card, which was quite a round. It's such a wonderful setting, a great golf course. Those dunes almost speak to you. "I could spend the rest of my days playing the 11th and never have a moment's regret."

ABOVE: *The 11th green on the Old Course.* **OPPOSITE:** *The green on the 10th hole at Ballybunion, with the 453-yard 11th hole stretching down the coastline in the distance.*

Irish links golf first appeared a full three hundred years after the game sprung up along the dunes of Scotland, but the Irish made up for lost time. Today, most golf travelers put at least one Irish links in their all-time top ten. And the grand dame of all Irish courses is the Ballybunion Old Course, on the southwest coast along the southern tip of the Shannon Estuary. Consistently ranked among the top courses in the world by every reputable golf publication, Ballybunion is a treeless masterpiece, woven through sand dunes and shaped by cool westerly winds and stinging, salty rain.

A conversation starter at any local pub is the question, "Who designed the course?" About the only points of agreement are that nine holes "appeared" in 1893 — "designed by God on the eighth day," somebody always says. The course expanded to eighteen holes in 1927, and architects Tom Simpson and Molly Gourlay were brought in for a redesign 1936. They tinkered here and there but left the bulk of the course exactly as they found it. "The beauty of the terrain surpasses that of any course we know," said Simpson. "Never for a moment did we imagine, or expect to find, such a really great course or such a glorious piece of golfing ground."

Ballybunion is now considered a national treasure and has become one of the most photographed golf holes in the world. Curving along the coastline with expansive views of the dunes, countryside, and the mountains of the Dingle Peninsula in the distance, the 11th is as visually arresting as it is challenging.

In 2000, the 11th wasn't so pretty for Sergio Garcia. The Spaniard held the early lead in the Irish Open at Ballybunion. But when the wind and rain picked up during the final on Sunday, Garcia had trouble standing on the 11th tee, much less hitting his shot. His tee shot found the high left rough, where he

---

"IF YOU'RE LUCKY ENOUGH TO MAKE PAR THERE, RUN TO THE BAR. FORGET ABOUT PLAYING THE REST OF THE GOLF COURSE. YOUR DAY WON'T GET ANY BETTER."

—CHRISTY O'CONNOR JR.

---

had no chance of reaching the green. After finding the rough again beside the green, Garcia finished with a 77 to fall out of contention. Even the winner, Sweden's Patrik Sjoland, was surprised by Garcia's play, saying, "I thought Sergio would get off to a fast start. But it didn't turn out that way, and I'm very glad of that."

The 11th is called "Watson's Favorite" after five-time British Open champion Tom Watson, who said, "It's the hole I admire and enjoy the most on a course I believe every golfer should try to play at least once." Watson added, "After playing Ballybunion for the first time a man would think that the game of golf originated here. There is a wild look to the place, the long grass covering the dunes that pitch and roll throughout the course, making it very intimidating. . . . Having played the Old Course in Ballybunion many times since my first visit in 1981, I am now of the opinion it is one of the best and most beautiful tests of links golf anywhere in the world." He'll get no argument from the locals.

BALLYBUNION OLD COURSE: 11TH HOLE DIAGRAM

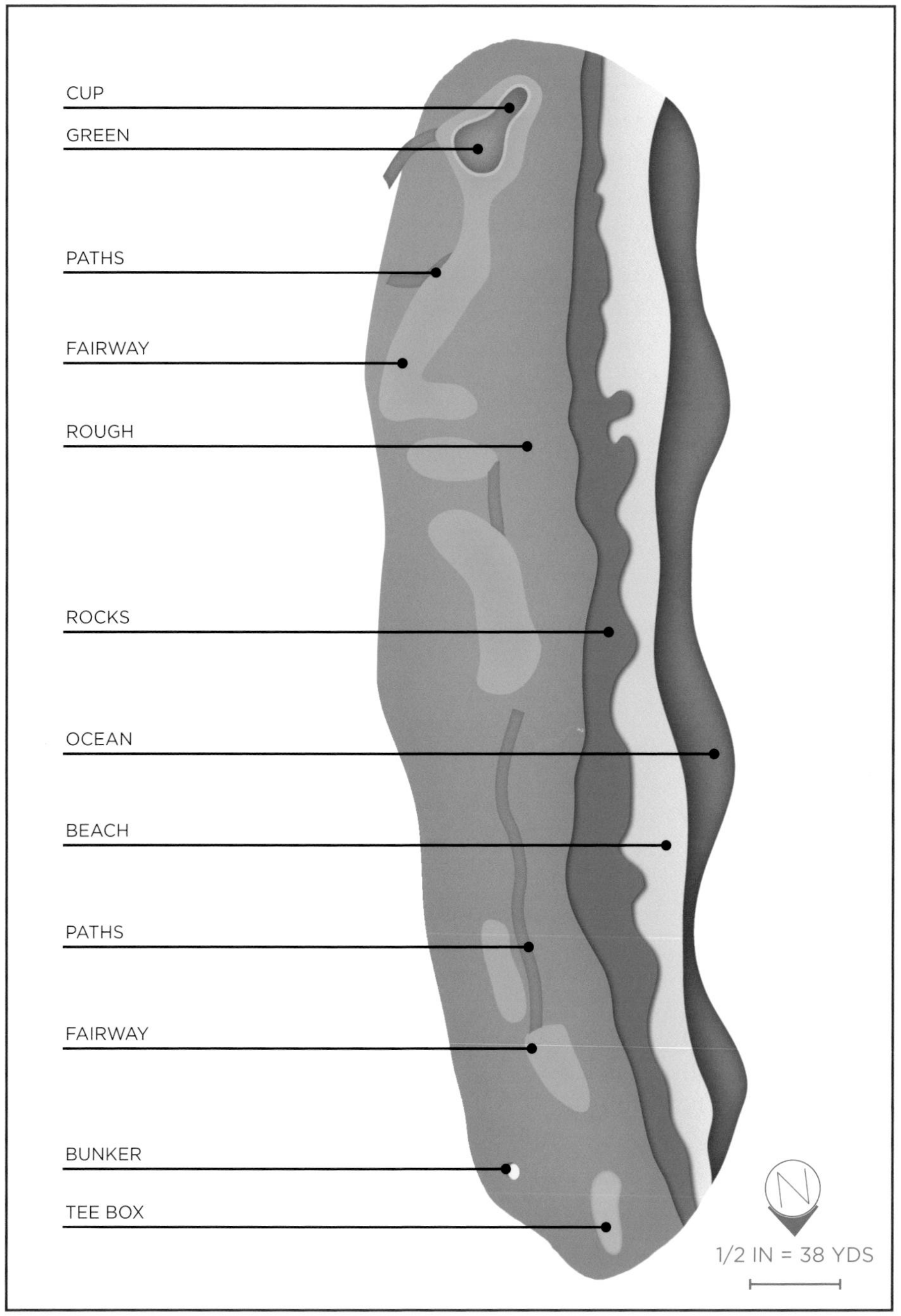

CUP
GREEN
PATHS
FAIRWAY
ROUGH
ROCKS
OCEAN
BEACH
PATHS
FAIRWAY
BUNKER
TEE BOX

1/2 IN = 38 YDS

OPPOSITE: *The green on the par-4 11th hole on the Ballybunion Old Course.*

"The 12th is one of the most amazing short holes in golf."

AUGUSTA NATIONAL GOLF CLUB
12th Hole

KEN VENTURI

One of the most respected men in golf, Hall of Famer Ken Venturi provided the golf world with a wealth of drama as a player, winning the 1964 U.S. Open while suffering through heatstroke and dehydration from the flu, an episode that almost killed him, and a feat that earned him Player of the Year honors that season. He had fifteen wins as a professional, but was also known as one of the last great amateurs, finishing second in the Masters in 1956 as an amateur after leading throughout the second and third rounds. Once he made the jump into the professional ranks, Venturi finished second in the Masters again in 1960.

After retiring from competition, he spent thirty years in the broadcast booth as the voice of golf for CBS, and was always brought in during the Masters at Augusta in Georgia for commentary on "Amen Corner," the stretch of holes that include 11, 12, and 13, three of the most difficult and dramatic in the game. Now retired and living in his native San Francisco, Venturi, who recovered from a debilitating stutter as a child, is a sought-after public speaker.

"The 12th at Augusta is one of the greatest short holes in the world, certainly the most dramatic in major championship golf. The most amazing situation at the 12th came in 1992 when Fred Couples hit the bank and his ball did not go in the water. I went back out there on Monday after Couples won, and I tried forever to keep a ball on that bank where his ball hung up, and I couldn't do it. How his ball stopped and didn't go in the water is a total miracle, because it can't be done. I was there and I tried and tried. I guess his ball rolled back into

the indentation it made when it hit the bank and that somehow kept it up, but balls just don't stay on that bank.

"It's a dramatic spot, but really for the wrong reasons. My line on the 12th hole — and it has been used many times — was always that you can lose the Masters on the 12th, but you can't win it on the 12th. When I played there, I

"IT'S A DRAMATIC SPOT, BUT REALLY FOR THE WRONG REASONS. MY LINE ON THE 12TH HOLE . . . WAS ALWAYS THAT YOU CAN LOSE THE MASTERS ON THE 12TH, BUT YOU CAN'T WIN IT ON THE 12TH."

—KEN VENTURI

---

probably had one of the best scoring averages ever on that hole because I didn't care where they put the pin: I always hit it in the middle of the green. As tempting as it might be, you just don't want to go for that pin. Put me in the middle of the green every time and you can cut the hole wherever you want it.

"The 12th is one of the most amazing short holes in golf, especially when you look at the differences in scores. People have made everything from a one to a 13 on that hole. You can take hard holes like the 16th at Cypress and get a huge disparity on scoring, but you don't always get that on a short hole. At the 12th at Augusta, you certainly do. It could be one of the most unique short holes of all of golf.

"You can't duplicate it, because you can't recreate the swirling winds of Amen Corner. When I played with Hogan for many years, he told me the secret to playing that hole. I can tell it now, because Hogan's gone. He told me at the time not to tell anybody. If you paid attention you would see that

Hogan would hit some shots at 12 quicker than others, so I finally asked him why he did that. It all had to do with the winds. He said, 'I never want to hit the shot while the flag is down,' meaning you couldn't feel the wind. 'If I hit it and then the wind comes up, I'm going to go in the water,' he said. 'I never hit my tee shot at 12 until I feel the wind on my cheek.' That made perfect sense. You can see how those winds swirl by looking at the flags at 11 and 12. They are really close together, but when one flag is up, the other is down. Hogan knew that, so he waited until he could feel the wind on his face before he would hit a shot there.

"You think about Amen Corner, 11 has been changed, they've made it longer, and 13 has been changed, but 12 is basically the same hole that Jones designed. When I was broadcasting at Augusta, I would always get called in on 12, because I could tell what the players were thinking. I'd been there and thought the same things. It was a hole made for shot-makers.

"I coined the phrase 'The Masters begins on the back nine on Sunday.' The 12th is a perfect example of what I meant by that."

Anyone who has turned on the television to watch a minute of the Masters has seen the 12th hole at Augusta National. The Hogan Bridge across Rae's Creek from the tee to the green of this picturesque par 3 is the opening shot of the CBS coverage. It's also the heart of what golfers know as "Amen Corner," a stretch of golf theater that begins in the center of the 11th fairway and extends through the tee shot at 13. Jack Nicklaus has called the 12th "the most difficult and demanding short hole in golf," and Tiger Woods said, "It's a hole where you have no room for error. If you try to get too much out of it, it can bite you."

OPPOSITE: *A scenic view of the water hazard guarding the 12th hole at Augusta National, December 1991.*

AUGUSTA NATIONAL GOLF CLUB: 12TH HOLE DIAGRAM

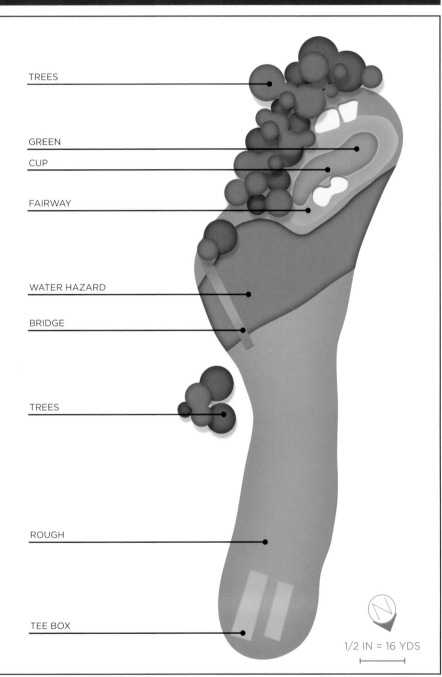

TREES

GREEN

CUP

FAIRWAY

WATER HAZARD

BRIDGE

TREES

ROUGH

TEE BOX

1/2 IN = 16 YDS

Greg Norman would certainly agree. Trying to win the Masters, a title he wanted more than any other and one that eluded him throughout his career, Norman held a 6-shot lead going into the final round in 1996, but when his tee shot found the water at 12, the lead and the title were gone. Nick Faldo won by 4. Norman contended again in 1999, pulling into the lead in the third round. But when he reached the 12th, his perfectly struck 8-iron shot sailed over the green and into the azaleas, dogwoods, and golden bells. A frantic search ensued, but Norman never found his ball. He went on to lose to José Maria Olazabal.

Fred Couples won the Masters in 1992 when his ball miraculously perched on the bank between the green and Rae's Creek, seeming to defy gravity and leading many to write that divine intervention played a role in his victory. The hole has also been a spot of great Masters levity. In 1949, Claude Harmon and Ben Hogan played the 12th in a combined three shots. Harmon hit first and made a hole-in-one. Hogan hit next, and put the shot to three feet. After making the birdie putt, Hogan walked to the 13th tee and said, "You know, Claude, I don't think I've ever birdied that hole before. What did you have?" Unfazed by his friend's obliviousness, Harmon said, "I had a one, Ben."

In the 1958 Masters, Ken Venturi thought he had played himself into a tie for the lead after Arnold Palmer made double bogey at the 12th. The only problem was that Palmer hadn't made 5: He'd actually made a 3. Palmer had the lead when he hit his tee shot over the green and the ball plugged. There was no embedded-ball rule on the books at the time, but Augusta National had instituted a local rule allowing players to lift, clean, and drop the ball when it embedded in its own pitchmark. Palmer declared his intentions to do just that, but the rules official on site, Arthur Lacey, shook his head and said, "You don't do that at Augusta."

Palmer played two balls, one from the pitchmark where he made a 5, and a second ball with a drop where he made par. It wasn't until three holes

OPPOSITE: *Overlooking the 12th green in Augusta National's Amen Corner.*

later that the rules committee convened and decided that Palmer had indeed made a par and not a double bogey. In the meantime, the 5 had gone up on the scoreboards and everyone, including Venturi, thought Palmer had dropped out of the lead. When the score was changed to a 3, Venturi was understandably miffed.

Venturi led again in 1960, when he stood in the Butler Cabin, where the awards ceremony is held, believing that he had won the Masters. No player had ever birdied the last two holes at Augusta National in the final round to win. But that's exactly what Palmer did to beat Venturi by one, a series of events that both men recall with vivid clarity almost a half-century later.

"Walking up the final fairway, having just hit maybe the finest club shot of my career to that point, I knew I now faced the biggest putt of my career," Palmer said of the 1960 win. "Even though I was probably as nervous as I'd ever been on a golf course, I knew I could make the putt." After the putt went in, Palmer leapt into the air, an image forever implanted in golf history, and one Ken Venturi, who saw it live from the Butler Cabin, will never forget.

Venturi would never don the green jacket, although he did win more than a few battles with Palmer, most notably in the 1964 Open. It was a Hall of Fame career, and one made even more impressive for the time in which he played, the heyday of Palmer and the dawn of Nicklaus. Winning any event in that era was a feat; winning fifteen times put Venturi in the company of the greatest in the game.

ABOVE: *Phil Mickelson hits his second shot on the 12th hole out of the bunker during the third round of the Masters Tournament, April 12, 2008.* **OPPOSITE:** *Tiger Woods in action on the 12th hole during the 2007 Masters, which he lost to Zach Johnson.*

SHINNECOCK HILLS GOLF CLUB
— *13th Hole* —

RAYMOND FLOYD

Hall of Famer Raymond Floyd won his fourth major championship title at Shinnecock Hills on Long Island, New York, when he captured the 1986 U.S. Open there. In so doing, the forty-five-year-old Floyd became the oldest winner in U.S. Open history. Three men shared the lead late in the final round of that championship, but Floyd was not among them. Then he birdied the 11th to pull within a shot of the lead, and when the other players faltered down the stretch Floyd made another birdie at the 13th to take a one-shot lead. He would make one more birdie at the 16th that afternoon to seal the victory, but it was the birdie at 13, one of Floyd's favorite holes in the world, that put him in the lead for good. He went on to become a member at the historic golf club, which was built in 1891, and he continues to play there every summer. Also a renowned architect, Floyd is one of the leading historians among players when it comes to classic golf course design.

"I don't know of a knowledgeable, good player anywhere who does not list Shinnecock among their top five courses in the world. It's a classic links course, and when you look down on it from above, every hole runs in a different direction, so it doesn't matter which way the wind is blowing, you're going to have to play all the shots. It is an incredibly special place, because when you think about how old that golf course is, most of the holes are basically the same as they were in the beginning, and yet it is still one of the greatest tests in the game.

SHINNECOCK HILLS GOLF CLUB: 13TH HOLE DIAGRAM

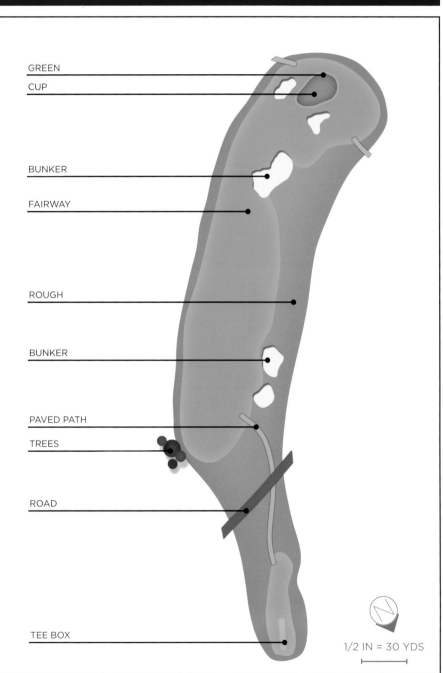

GREEN

CUP

BUNKER

FAIRWAY

ROUGH

BUNKER

PAVED PATH

TREES

ROAD

TEE BOX

1/2 IN = 30 YDS

OPPOSITE: *The 13th green at Shinnecock Hills Golf Club.*

"Number 13, specifically, has never been lengthened or modified since the 1930s. It's an outstanding-looking hole, because it's the highest point on the golf course, and when you stand on that tee looking out at that vista and everything that surrounds the golf course, it takes your breath away.

"The green sits up and is well protected by bunkering left and right, and the falloff right and back is significant. You can't miss right. The mounding on

> "WHEN I WON THERE IN 1986, I KNEW
> ENOUGH TO STAY AWAY FROM THAT FAIRWAY
> BUNKER AND I PLAYED SAFELY TO THE
> MIDDLE OF THE GREEN, SO I COULD 2-PUTT
> AND GET OUT OF THERE WITH A PAR."
>
> —RAYMOND FLOYD

the left, which was pretty natural behind the left bunker coming down to the green, is why they had to get some soil from that architectural bunker, to lift that green up.

"It's a rewarding hole in that you can birdie it. But if you make one bad shot, whether it's the tee shot or the second, or you get on the wrong side of the green and you 3-putt it, it can get you. It has lots of ways to bite you, but it will reward you.

"I love the hole. When I won there in 1986, I knew enough to stay away from that fairway bunker and I played safely to the middle of the green, so I could 2-putt and get out of there with a par. Yes, it can be a birdie hole, but it's a hole that can ruin your round if you make the slightest little mistake.

"That's so typical of the great old golf holes from the best architects. You know, when you go back to the early days of golf in this country — turn of the

last century through the '30s and even up until the '50s — we could name all the great golf course architects, and their work is still considered untouchable. But one of the reasons for that is the fact that those guys didn't take criticism. To paraphrase Donald Ross, *there is no such thing as fair or unfair in golf.* If there is a hazard or other obstacle, it's the player's job to negotiate it. That's part of the game. I think modern architects take too much criticism to heart, people saying, 'this hole's unfair,' or 'that hazard shouldn't be there,' or 'this hole is too hard,' that it has diluted a lot of the greatness and a lot of the creativity we see in older courses like Shinnecock. An architect's job is to challenge the player, but also to have everyone finish the round having had some fun.

"That is what's so much fun about Shinnecock: Everything is straight-forward. There is no trickiness, but once you've played it two or three times, you see subtleties that come to you. Being a member and having been out here every summer, it's amazing what I've learned over time.

"To me, it's the greatest golf course in the world, and the 13th is one of the best holes on it."

———————————————————

Rolling through the windswept sand dunes of Southampton, New York, Shinnecock Hills is the closest thing there is in America to classic links golf, and is as close to golf perfection as can be found anywhere. The course was originally built in 1891 by a small construction team that included 150 Native Americans of the Shinnecock Nation. The clubhouse, which still stands today, opened a year later. The club was an original charter member of the United States Golf Association, and the first club in America to allow women as members, beginning from the day it opened its doors. Since then it has hosted four U.S. Opens in three different centuries, producing some of the greatest drama in the history of the game.

In 1995, Corey Pavin won the U.S. Open, his only major title, by shooting a final-round 68 at Shinnecock in a nip-and-tuck battle with Greg Norman. Then in 2004, Shinnecock bared her teeth, becoming the hardest U.S. Open course in modern history. The average score for the week was 78.7, and only two players finished under par. The winner, Retief Goosen, had eleven one-putt greens in the final round, one of which came at the difficult 13th hole.

Goosen missed the green to the right at 13, leaving himself with a difficult chip to a sloping and lightning-fast green in Sunday's final round face-off with Phil Mickelson. A hundred pros would have had trouble getting the ball up and down under benign circumstances. With the pressure of the U.S. Open on the line, the shot was next to impossible. But Goosen managed to pull it off, chipping the ball to within 10 feet of the hole and draining the putt for another crucial par, one he would need down the stretch to hold off Mickelson and win his second U.S. Open title.

In classic links style, nothing about Shinnecock Hills is overpowering, but every hole presents players with multiple options. The par-4 13th, a deceptively short 370-yard dogleg with spectacular views, is visually deceiving from the beginning as the tee box lines the player up at an odd angle. A strategic fairway bunker lies to the right at about 285 yards, and from there the hole narrows and doglegs to the right. A player who tries to fly the bunker must do so into an ever-narrowing landing area. Laying back brings the bunker into play and forces a longer second shot into an elevated and well-guarded green with bunkers and mounds on either side. Strategy, not strength, is the key to negotiating the course, and nowhere is that more evident than on 13.

OPPOSITE: *A view of the 13th green at Shinnecock Hills.*

MUIRFIELD VILLAGE
14th Hole

Kenny Perry has been one of the game's steadiest performers for two decades. He has won thirteen times on the PGA Tour and finished second in playoffs in major championships twice. He also helped secure the 2008 Ryder Cup for the U.S. team, defeating Henrik Stenson in the singles matches. Now content to stay home with his family and operate the public golf course he built with his father, Perry remains the same easygoing Kentuckian he was when he first turned pro.

KENNY PERRY

"The 14th at Muirfield Village is my favorite hole in the game, and one of the best short par 4's on tour. A lot of people point to the 10th at Riviera as a great short 4, but I think the 14th at Muirfield Village [in Dublin, Ohio] is much more of a precision shot-maker's hole. You've got a long, narrow green that moves away from you with a creek on the right and a bunker to the left. It looks like your bailout is left, but if you hit it in that bunker the green slopes away from you, and it's almost impossible to keep a pitch shot on the green.

"When I won there in 2008, I hit it long and left on Sunday and hit one of the great pitches of my life — one of those flop shots and it trickled down there for a tap-in par. When you look at it, you don't think about it as being much of a hole. You hit a 3-iron or something off the tee to get it 225 to 250 [yards] down there, but you have a little creek up the left side and rough on the right. Some of the monster hitters like J. B. Holmes or Bubba Watson or

maybe John Daly think about hitting it over the creek and up there close to the green, but the majority of the players lay back short.

"Your first instinct is that it should be a birdie hole, but the more you play it the more you realize you can get in a lot of trouble, and you say to yourself, 'I need to try to get four pars and move on to the next hole.' On Sundays, when they have the pin back right, you've got about a five-foot area to hit it in. You can't go left; you can't go right; you can't go long. So even though you're hitting a short iron, you have got to pick the right number, be confident in that number, and be able to hit it. It is a precision golf hole. You definitely have to hit it straight. Just a little bit right-to-left off the tee and it's in the water.

"EVEN THOUGH YOU'RE HITTING A SHORT IRON, YOU HAVE GOT TO PICK THE RIGHT NUMBER, BE CONFIDENT IN THAT NUMBER, AND BE ABLE TO HIT IT."

—RAYMOND FLOYD

"Every time I see Jack [Nicklaus] — you know, he's been my Presidents Cup captain a couple of times — I always give him a hug and thank him for Muirfield Village. That's the place where I made it. I got my first win there in 1991. I think it's the greatest golf course we play. Yes, I've had success there, won there three times, but it's also a fantastic golf course. I understand what Jack was thinking there, what strategy is required there, and what shots you need to play.

"Fourteen is my favorite hole on my favorite course. In my opinion, it's one of the best anywhere."

MUIRFIELD VILLAGE: 14TH HOLE DIAGRAM

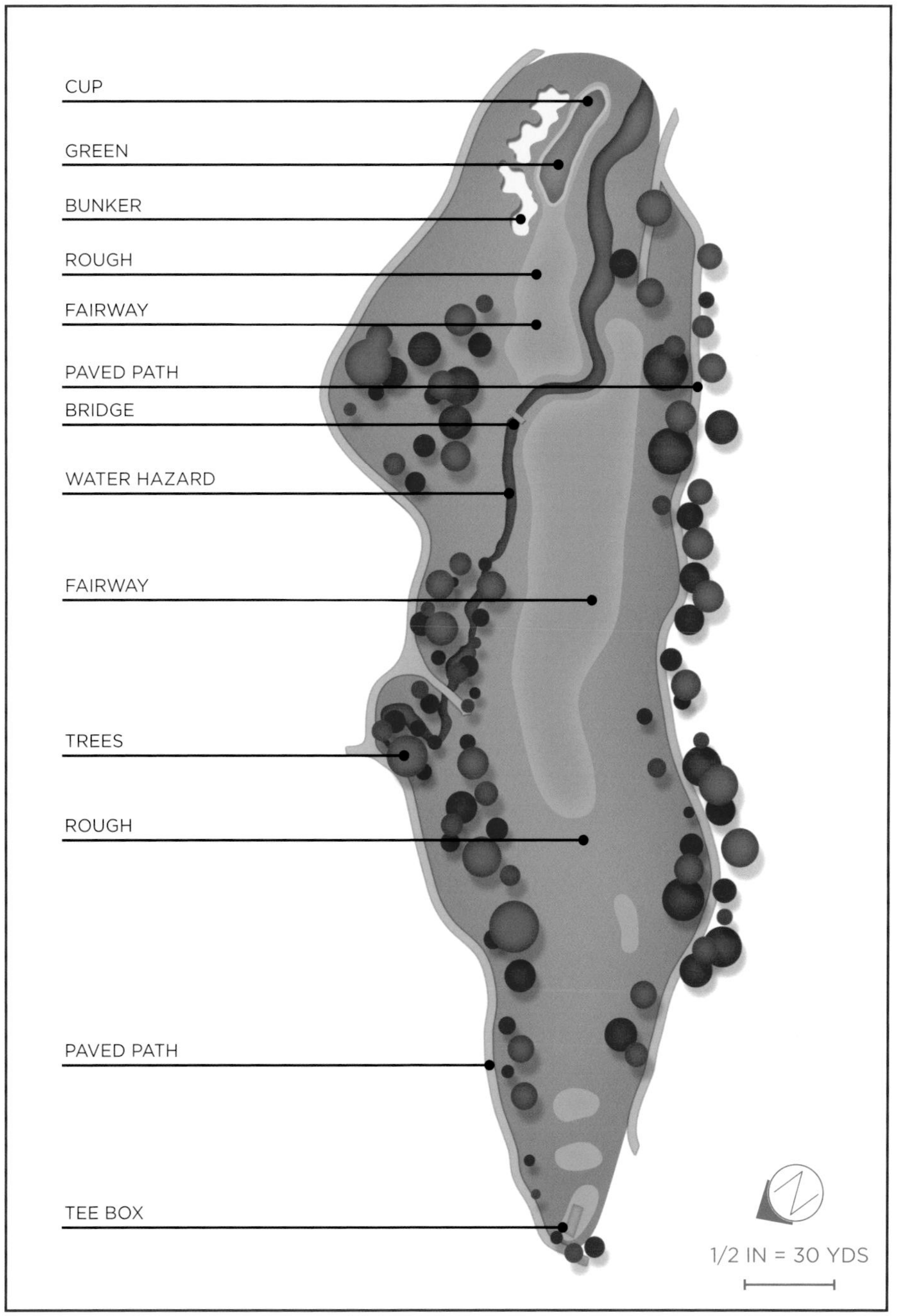

CUP
GREEN
BUNKER
ROUGH
FAIRWAY
PAVED PATH
BRIDGE
WATER HAZARD
FAIRWAY
TREES
ROUGH
PAVED PATH
TEE BOX

1/2 IN = 30 YDS

OPPOSITE: *Kenny Perry hits his approach shot from the 14th fairway during the final round of the Memorial Tournament at Muirfield Village, June 1, 2008.*

Jack Nicklaus has a well-earned reputation as one of the most analytical players in the game, and that genius is evident in his design masterpiece, Muirfield Village, which hosts Nicklaus's annual Memorial Tournament. Eight Hall of Famers have won the Memorial, including Nicklaus himself, in 1977 and 1984. Tom Watson also won it twice, as did Greg Norman. But only two people have won the tournament three times: Tiger Woods and Kenny Perry. Both those players owe their victories to their play at the shortest par 4 on the course, the treacherous 14th.

With a stream running diagonally in front of the green, along with bunkers and willow trees, this is the kind of hole Donald Ross had in mind when he said, "In holes of this length both the drive and approach should be difficult, otherwise they are usually very uninteresting." A lot of words have been used to describe Nicklaus's crown jewel, but "uninteresting" is not among them. It is a thinking man's hole that has produced some of the greatest drama on tour. In two of Tiger's consecutive victories in 2000 and 2001, he pulled his approach shot left of the narrow green, leaving himself one of the most difficult pitch shots on the course. The green falls away from the player here, with a creek just beyond. On both occasions, Tiger opened the face of his wedge and took a full swing, shooting the ball straight up in the air. Both times, the ball landed

softly, trickled along the putting surface, and found the cup for birdie. From a spot where normal mortals would make no better than bogey, Tiger played the hole under par, and added another extraordinary moment to his expanding highlight reel.

It's almost puzzling that the hole creates such dramatic play. It appears benign. But those who fail to lay up in the right spot and retain complete command of their short irons are likely to walk away with a big number. According to Nicklaus, "Most players who come unglued on the second shot do so because they have let the narrowness and the length of the green relative to the severity of the hazards — water right, sand left — over-intimidate them. Avoid that tendency and your good approach will be rewarded with a relatively easy birdie putt."

Nobody understood the perils of the 14th better than Kenny Perry, who picked up his first career tour win at the Memorial, and then landed his most important victory there in 2008, a triumph that secured Perry a spot on the winning Ryder Cup team. "That was my number-one goal, and I made no bones about it," Perry said. "I really hung myself out there, because I put all my eggs in that Ryder Cup basket, but it was being played at Valhalla, in my home state [of Kentucky], and I wanted that to be the swan song of my career, to make my career, really." Getting to that goal required a win. On his favorite hole, and on a course he loves more than any on tour, Perry came through.

ABOVE: *Tiger Woods and Ernie Els finishing up on the 14th green during the first round of the Memorial Tournament, June 4, 2009.* **OPPOSITE:** *The 14th green at Muirfield Village.*

"You can't get away with anything other than perfect shots."

AUGUSTA NATIONAL GOLF CLUB
15th Hole

ZACH JOHNSON

A no-nonsense Midwesterner, Zach Johnson is always on point, never shying away from expressing himself, but never feeling the need to interject his opinions without being asked. He won six times in five years, including a victory over Tiger Woods at the 2007 Masters in Augusta, Georgia, and is considered one of the toughest young contenders in the game. He has the courtly manners one would expect of a family man from Cedar Rapids. He also errs on the side of understatement — in his dress, demeanor, and the words he chooses, but not in his golf game.

"Fifteen at Augusta is a great, great par 5, reachable but always challenging. Of course it's been lengthened over time to keep up with the changes in the game, but it probably plays now about the same length it did seventy-five years ago given the equipment and conditions back then. Today, if you hope to go for the green in two you need to hit a tee shot down the right center. That's not as easy as it looks since from the tee it's slightly uphill, but once you crest the hill the second shot is severely downhill. For me, if I'm going to try to go for the green, I need a 5-wood or a long iron.

"If I'm not going for the green, the layup shot in front of the water depends solely on where the pin is located. The left side of the fairway down at the bottom near the water seems a little more level than the right side. But the third shot, if you lay up, is always going to be severely downhill with

AUGUSTA NATIONAL GOLF CLUB: 15TH HOLE DIAGRAM

GREEN
CUP
BUNKER
WATER HAZARD
TREES
FAIRWAY
ROUGH
TREES
TEE BOX

1/2 IN = 38 YDS

a wedge. If the pin is on the left side of the green, I like to lay up center to a little right-center, even though the slope of the fairway is a little steeper there. At least from there you have more green to work with. If the pin is on the right, then obviously I want to be on the left side of the fairway and hit my wedge shot in. The green is almost a tabletop. It's very hard and very fast.

"Being able to control your spin and the trajectory of your shot is always at a premium with your wedge from there. It is very easy to hit the ball almost into the center of the green with too much spin and have it come back, sometimes even off the front and into the water. Or you can carry it a little too far and be off the back, which is not good. Everything slopes down toward the water, so from behind the green you're chipping uphill to a hard, fast green that runs away from you with water on the other side. That can be tough.

"It's a birdie hole, definitely, because if you're standing in the fairway with a 5-wood or a long iron in your hand, you feel like you can always hit it into that right-hand trap and still have a play. Even if you don't hit the green, from that trap you have a chance to get it up and down.

"It's just a great hole: a great risk/reward par 5 and one where you can't get away with anything other than perfect shots."

In designing one of the most scenic "straight" par 5's in the world, with the tee shot cresting a hill and the second shot playing down to a green that is guarded by water, Alister MacKenzie set out to create one of the most spectacular cathedral settings in the game — and no one questions his success. In addition to being breathtaking, the 15th at Augusta National has been the site of some of the game's greatest competition since the club first opened in 1932. Lengthened and changed over the years, the 15th remains the spot where Masters hopefuls rise and fall. MacKenzie described the original intent of the hole as "not only an interesting 3-shot hole, as one will

OPPOSITE: *Looking over the 15th hole at Augusta National Golf Club.*

be maneuvering for position from the tee shot onward, but also a magnificent 2-shot hole, as a skillful and courageous player will, aided by a large hillock to the right, be able to pull his second shot around to the green."

No more perfect second shot was ever pulled off than the one struck by Jack Nicklaus in 1986. At age forty-six, Nicklaus was considered to be well past his prime, but after four birdies on the back nine, he was in the midst of the most unlikely charge in major championship history: four shots back with four to play. His tee shot on 15 found the center of the fairway, cresting

---

"THE GREEN IS ALMOST A TABLETOP. IT'S VERY HARD AND VERY FAST. BEING ABLE TO CONTROL YOUR SPIN AND THE TRAJECTORY OF YOUR SHOT IS ALWAYS AT A PREMIUM WITH YOUR WEDGE FROM THERE."

—ZACH JOHNSON

---

the hill perfectly. From there, Nicklaus took out a 3-iron, turned to his son Jackie and said, "How much good do you think a 3 would do?" Jackie didn't answer, even after the shot found the green. But when the 20-foot eagle putt went in, Jackie leapt with his fists skyward as the crowd erupted. Fifteen minutes later, Seve Ballesteros was standing in the middle of the 15th fairway with a similar shot to the one Nicklaus had earlier, only a little closer to the green. But Ballesteros had to wait for the group ahead to clear the green, and for the crowd to calm down after Nicklaus made his eagle putt at 15 and hit a tee shot at 16 to within a foot. With all the commotion, and the pressure of the situation, Ballesteros hooked his second shot into the water at 15 just as Nicklaus was tapping in for birdie at 16. By nightfall Nicklaus would

become the oldest Masters winner ever and the only man in history to win eighteen professional majors.

Eleven years after Nicklaus's memorable win, history was made again as Tiger Woods became the youngest man to win the Masters and the first man of color to capture a major championship. In the process he set a dozen Masters records. He also hit 8- and 9-irons into the 15th green all four days of the tournament, turning what had once been a lengthy par 5 into a short par 4. In the final, he reached the green with a driver and a 9-iron, prompting major changes in the hole. The members at Augusta National attempted to "Tiger-proof" 15 by adding more length, taking down many of the mounds on the right side of the fairway, and adding trees.

According to Tiger, "It's a lot different. They've added a lot of length, which is going to make it a lot harder to hit the green in 2, and that's actually going to help the long hitters. Some of the short hitters who could use the mounds on the right on 15, they're not there now, so they'll be hitting 3-woods or 4-woods or long irons in there. With the new trees, you have to pick a different line off the tee, which sets you up a little differently for your second shot. So, it's tougher."

One of those short hitters who had to play the 15th differently was Zach Johnson. In fact, the Iowa native showed up for the 2007 Masters with a very simple game plan, which he admitted to at the beginning of the week and never varied from throughout: No matter where he drove the ball on the par 5's, he would lay up and let his wedge game carry him. There would be no temptations and no second-guessing. That strategy paid off: Johnson played Augusta's par 5's 11-under-par for the week. He also birdied the 15th on Sunday for a closing 69, finishing two shots ahead of Tiger to clinch his first major championship.

OPPOSITE: *The 15th hole at Augusta National in 1989, before it was lengthened and altered.*

CYPRESS POINT CLUB
— *16th Hole* —

JERRY PATE

Jerry Pate is known for great shots at dramatic moments: the 5-iron from the rough to within a foot of the final hole to win the U.S. Open; the approach at the final hole in the inaugural Players Championship at TPC Sawgrass; and at the Bing Crosby National Pro-Am, the only tournament hole-in-one ever recorded at the 16th at Cypress Point in Monterey, California. A native of Pensacola, Florida and an All-American at the University of Alabama, Pate is one of the only players to win the U.S. Amateur and U.S. Open in back-to-back years. He is also a renowned golf course architect, scholar of the game, and regular analyst for the BBC — the kind of man who can hold court in any clubhouse in the world.

"I would say the 16th at Cypress Point is one of the most famous holes in the world. Obviously the [par 5] 18th hole at Pebble Beach gets television exposure every year during the AT&T Pebble Beach National Pro-Am, and sure, the holes at Augusta National, especially in Amen Corner, get recognition every year, but there is no question that 16 at Cypress is the most famous par 3 in the world, especially for those who are students of the game.

"There is no other hole like it. It's on the prettiest piece of property in America. You've got Carmel Bay on one side and Monterey Bay on the other. Even if you never hit a golf shot, you can stand on the 16th tee and have one of the greatest outdoor experiences of your life just based on the sheer beauty of the place. You can watch the whales migrate during the winter months, and

105

the big seals. It's almost surreal that this sort of thing exists in America, and to have a golf hole that plays across that is absolutely magnificent.

"Most of the time when the wind blows it comes from the southwest so that it's right into you. [Alister] MacKenzie gave you an option to lay up to the left and then wedge on, but for the high handicapper, even the layup is a pretty good carry, about 150 yards over water. You have the short 15th that precedes it, where you play a 140-yard approach to an accessible concave green where the ball tends to kick toward the center from all sides. Then you walk over to 16 and you say, 'Oh my goodness,' because now it's 230 yards from the back tee.

"Back when the course was first built, that was a full driver shot. Ben Hogan never went for the green during the tournament. He always laid up to the left and chipped on. Back then, a person who could really play could only hit a tee shot about 230 with that equipment, notwithstanding the elements. If the wind and rain were blowing in on you, almost everybody would have to lay up. In good conditions, average players could not reach the green. So it's definitely a challenging hole, always has been.

"In 1982, I was playing with Peter Jacobsen, Jack Lemmon, and Jim Walter, who ran the Jim Walter Corporation out of Tampa. Waiting on the tee with us were Jack Nicklaus, President Ford, and Tom Watson. It was almost a make-believe group. The wind was blowing in a little from right to left, but it was a pretty calm day, comparatively. I had a Wilson Staff 1-iron and a No. 1 orange ProStaff ball, and it was sort of unique that I was playing a No. 1 ball. So, I hit the shot, and it was right on line the entire way. The ball hit the green, bounced twice, and went in for a hole-in-one.

"It was certainly a shot that I'll remember the rest of my life. There haven't been a lot of holes-in-one on that hole. Not long afterward, I gave the 1-iron and the ball to the Cypress Point Club. Now they're mounted in a walnut case in the clubhouse, so everybody can see them and hear the story."

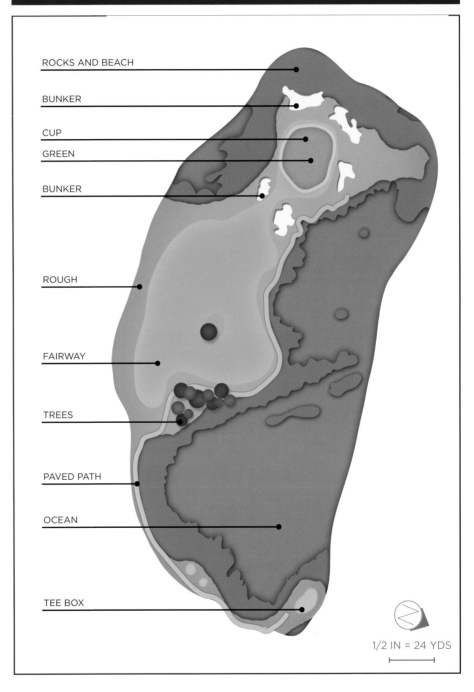

CYPRESS POINT CLUB: 16TH HOLE DIAGRAM

ROCKS AND BEACH

BUNKER

CUP

GREEN

BUNKER

ROUGH

FAIRWAY

TREES

PAVED PATH

OCEAN

TEE BOX

1/2 IN = 24 YDS

OPPOSITE: *A scenic view of the action on the 16th hole at Cypress Point during the 1981 Bing Crosby National Pro-Am.*

On the card, the architects of Cypress Point are Seth Raynor and Alister MacKenzie, two of the early twentieth century's greats with such masterworks as Golf Club of Chicago and Augusta National to their credit. But when it came to the cliffs of Monterey, where Cypress Point abuts the sea, Raynor and MacKenzie's main goal was to not screw up what God had put in front of them.

"EVEN IF YOU NEVER HIT A GOLF SHOT, YOU CAN STAND ON THE 16TH TEE AND HAVE ONE OF THE GREATEST OUTDOOR EXPERIENCES OF YOUR LIFE JUST BASED ON THE SHEER BEAUTY OF THE PLACE."

—JERRY PATE

The club was the brainchild of Marion Hollins, a child of Wall Street privilege whose father, Harry, was an investment partner and close friend of William Vanderbilt and J. P. Morgan. Growing up on a Long Island estate, Hollins played sports to keep up with her brothers. Her aptitude and love of golf led her to win the U.S. Women's amateur title in 1921. Two years after that victory, she accepted a job as the athletic director at the new Pebble Beach Resort, where her gilded East Coast contacts made her an invaluable asset. But Hollins, who was also considered the greatest horsewoman of the 1920s, soon ventured out in search of a new challenge, and found one a mile north of Pebble Beach on 150 acres of land the Spanish settlers had dubbed "La Punta de Cipreses."

Optioning the land for $1,000 an acre, Hollins hired Raynor to create the Cypress Point Club. But when it came to the spectacular craggy cliffs at the property's edge, Raynor feared that the par-3 16th that Hollins envisioned would be far too much for the average player. According to MacKenzie, who stepped in after Raynor's untimely death, "Except for minor details in construction, I was in no way responsible for the hole. It was largely due to the vision of Miss Marion Hollins. It was suggested to her by the late Seth Raynor that it was a pity the carry over the ocean was too long to enable a hole to be designed on this particular site. Miss Hollins said she did not think it was an impossible carry. She then teed up a ball and drove to the middle of the site for the suggested green." The architects built the hole exactly to Hollins's specifications and its legend took hold soon after.

The 16th is now the most famous par 3 in the world, and deservedly so. With waves crashing on black stones in front and behind, the green looks like a coffee table perched amid five white bunkers and a sliver of green grass. To the left is a bailout area with a lone cypress standing guard.

For decades, Cypress Point was part of the three-course rotation for the "Crosby Clambake," later known as the Bing Crosby National Pro-Am and then the AT&T Pebble Beach National Pro-Am, and the 16th was always the most talked-about hole of the event. In 1954, Ed "Porky" Oliver took sixteen strokes on the par 3, but that record only stood for five years. In 1959, a club pro from Ohio named Hans Merrell made a 19, which is sixteen strokes over par: the highest over-par score ever recorded on a single hole in a PGA Tour event. Remarkably, Merrell never hit a shot in the water. He spent most of his time on the beach, hacking through clumps of ice plant below the thirty-foot cliff.

Of all the famous shots, perhaps none is more lasting than the hole-in-one by Jerry Pate, a moment captured on canvas by the greatest sports artist in history, Leroy Neiman, and a shot that remains a topic of conversation in golf circles everywhere.

OPPOSITE: *An aerial view of the 16th hole. The highest score recorded here was a 19 in 1959.*

THE OLD COURSE AT ST. ANDREWS
— *17th Hole* —

JACK NICKLAUS

There is no greater champion than Jack Nicklaus. The winner of eighteen professional majors and two U.S. Amateur titles, he is in a league of his own. For five decades, the Nicklaus name has been synonymous with the best in golf. Now one of the most prolific architects in the game, Nicklaus continues to stand apart. He has won tournaments around the world and designed courses on every continent except Antarctica, but St. Andrews in Scotland holds a special place in his heart.

"The 17th at St. Andrews is incredible, and one of the best holes in golf because of what it is and where it is, the history of it, and the sense of place. The Old Course to me is a very special place just because of how it relates to the history of the game of golf. I suppose if you took St. Andrews and put it somewhere else it would be just another golf course. But because it's in Scotland, and because of what it means to the game of golf, it becomes something very special.

"I go back to 1959 when my father and I were over there for the Walker Cup matches. My dad came over with three of his friends, and they played St. Andrews while we [the Walker Cup team] were at Muirfield. He came back from his round, and I said, 'How did you enjoy St. Andrews?' He said, 'What an awful golf course! Boy, there are bumps all over the place.' Of course he's an American, and had never played on anything like that. It was the

first round of golf he ever played over there, and with all those bumps, he thought the greens were terrible. How in the world did anybody ever putt those things?

"So five years later when I came back, I didn't know how I was going to like the course because of what my dad had said. But I fell in love with the place the first day I played it. I loved the opening tee shot, and it got better from there. I've always loved it. I don't know all the bunkers, obviously, but I know a fair number of them and can name fifteen or twenty of them. There's nothing like them — from the way they're placed

---

"THE 17TH AT ST. ANDREWS REQUIRES YOU TO PLAY GOOD GOLF."

—JACK NICKLAUS

---

and where they are to the shot values that you have with them. Of course, the bunkering is very difficult. There are a lot of bunkers out there, and when you're in them you're not going to get out of them going forward. And the greens are really tough, too. That's what makes it. You don't play any other golf course like this one. There's just no other course that is even remotely close.

"The 17th is a really hard hole. There are the old railway sheds that you used to have to drive the ball over [before the Old Course Hotel was built] and the green that sits in there has the road to the right and the bunker to the left. It's really a par 4½. That's the way to look at it, not that it has the length of being a par 4½, but it has the shot values of a par 4½. I play it to the front and take my chances with par. If you challenge the road or challenge the Road Bunker, you've probably made a mistake.

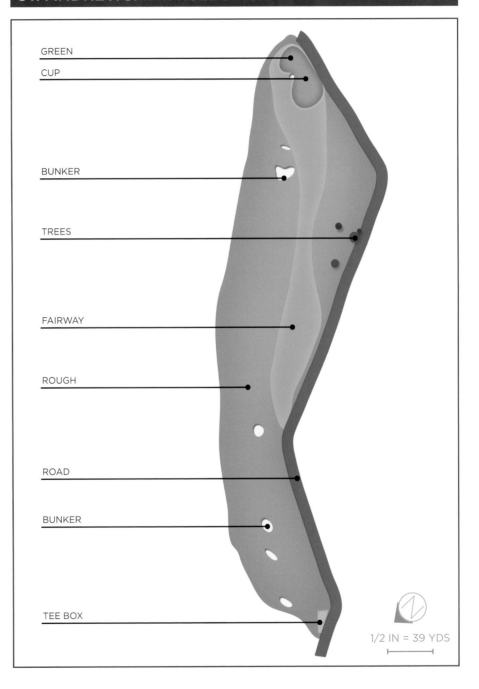

THE OLD COURSE AT ST. ANDREWS: 17TH HOLE DIAGRAM

GREEN

CUP

BUNKER

TREES

FAIRWAY

ROUGH

ROAD

BUNKER

TEE BOX

1/2 IN = 39 YDS

OPPOSITE: *The world-famous Swilcan Bridge crossing the Swilcan Burn at St. Andrews. The Old Course Hotel stands in the background, overlooking the 17th hole.*

"It's just a fantastic hole, because a lot of holes that have a lot of history don't necessarily require good golf. The 17th at St. Andrews requires you to play good golf."

———————————————————

Designed by God with a little help from various kings and lords over the years, the 17th at the Old Course at St. Andrews, dubbed "the Road Hole" for the narrow road along its right side, has been beguiling golfers since the 1500s. A dogleg right with a blind tee shot over what was once a barn and is now the Old Course Hotel, the hole gives the player numerous options — none of them pleasant. The safe play is to hit the tee shot left, but that makes the green unreachable. A drive played too far right caroms over a stone wall and out of bounds. But making a properly placed tee shot to a narrow sliver of

fairway is actually the easy part. The second shot to a slender, oblique, and crowned green is made even more difficult by the pit of sand in front known as the Road Bunker and by the road itself that runs to the right of the green. A pulled second shot is destined for the bunker, from which any number but par can be made, and anything right or long will end up on the gravel road.

In 1984, Tom Watson tried to go for the flag on the 17th with a 2-iron, but his approach hit the backside of the green and scooted onto the road, finishing only a foot from the stone wall that separates the course from the town. Watson played a ricochet shot off the wall and back to the course, but he made bogey and lost the British Open by a single shot.

"Links golf, when you play it, requires a different skill set," Tom Watson said in 2009. "Those skills are ones of touch and feel that may not be used all the time when you play American-type golf courses. The Road Hole . . . doesn't make much of a difference to me because I always make bogey on that son of a gun anyway. I always make my 5, get out of there, and go

ABOVE: *Jack Nicklaus drives a shot during the 1970 British Open at St. Andrews, as spectators and other golfers watch. Gary Player can be seen left of center in a white shirt.*
OPPOSITE: *The Road Bunker on the 17th hole, 2008.*

ahead. A par there is a like a birdie. Five's not a bad score on the Road Hole any time."

Many other professionals have failed to land even a 5 there. In 1978, Japan's Tommy Nakajima tried to putt his third shot around the bunker, but the contours gobbled his ball into the pit. Four sand shots and a couple of putts later, Nakajima walked away with a 9, leading the British press to dub the bunker, "The Sands of Nakajima." Headline writers were equally creative in 2000 when Native American player Notah Begay, then tied for the lead in the British Open, pulled his approach at 17 so badly that it bounded off the hardpan and ended

---

"THE ROAD HOLE . . . DOESN'T MAKE MUCH OF A DIFFERENCE TO ME BECAUSE I ALWAYS MAKE BOGEY ON THAT SON OF A GUN ANYWAY. I ALWAYS MAKE MY 5, GET OUT OF THERE, AND GO AHEAD. A PAR THERE IS A LIKE A BIRDIE."

— TOM WATSON

---

up on the Swilcan Burn, a walled stream running through the course. When Begay took off his shoes and attempted to play the ball from the shallow water, the tabloid headlines read: "Have-a-go Navajo Gets His Feet Burned." Later that same week, David Duval saw his challenge to Tiger Woods come to an end in the Road Bunker when three shots failed to extricate him. Duval was finally forced to play backward, ending his chances of victory.

Tiger Woods understands the challenges presented by the Road Hole and he continues to give it all due respect. "You have to be careful there," Woods said. "You have to pick your line depending on the wind and not get

too aggressive or you could hit it in the bunker, where you don't want to be, or on the road."

The 2009 British Open champion, Stewart Cink, called the 17th "architectural genius. When you first play it, you don't understand the brilliance behind it, but the more you play there, the more you understand that St. Andrews allows you to hit it as far left as you want, but that's not the optimum way to play the hole. The approaches get narrower, and the greens get shallower the farther left you go. To open up the approaches and give yourself the best chance of getting close, you have to play to the right where all the trouble is. The 17th is the perfect example of that. You can play to the left, and it becomes almost a par 5. To make a par or have a chance at birdie, you have to play as close to the trouble on the right as possible the entire way."

Nearly forty years earlier, 1960s golf champion Gary Player called it a "devilish hole," and fifty years before that, in 1910, the great golf writer Bernard Darwin wrote of the Road Hole: "The 17th hole has been more praised and abused probably than any other hole in the world. It has been called unfair, and by many harder names as well; it has caused champions with a predilection for pitching rather than running to tear their hair; it has certainly ruined an infinite number of scores. Many like it, most respect it, and all fear it."

None respect and appreciate it more than Jack Nicklaus, who won the Open Championship at St. Andrews in 1970 and again in 1978. When Nicklaus turned sixty-five in 2005, he made his final appearance in the Open Championship at St. Andrews, an appearance that prompted an unprecedented move: The Royal Bank of Scotland issued a five-pound note with Nicklaus's image on the back, the first time in history that a person other than the British monarch was depicted. It was an honor that remains unmatched.

OPPOSITE: *Looking over the 17th green toward the town of St. Andrews.*

"One of the most difficult and intimidating holes you'll ever play."

PEBBLE BEACH GOLF LINKS
— *18th Hole* —

PETER JACOBSEN

Peter Jacobsen is a big fan of Pebble Beach: It was the scene of his triumphant finish at the 1995 AT&T National Pro-Am, when he held off David Duval to win. In addition, Jacobsen is one of the most respected commentators and architects in golf. He was the tour's "Comeback Player of the Year" in 2003 after winning in Hartford, and has twenty-two total wins as a professional.

He is also one of the wittiest and most charming men in the game, a consummate entertainer, speaker, and musician. The justly famous Pebble Beach in Monterey, California, remains his favorite course in the world, with the 18th his most loved and respected finishing hole in the game.

"Obviously, given the setting, the 18th at Pebble Beach is one of the most visually spectacular holes on the planet, and one of the all-time great closing holes in all of golf.

"The reason the 18th is so appealing and so beautiful is that it puts you right on the edge of the coastline. You tee off from this spectacular tee block that, literally, hangs out over the ocean. You play over the ocean to a sliver of land that looks like it's also hanging out over the sea. You want to stand on that tee with a lot of confidence, but that's difficult with all the shifting winds. There's not much room for error. There is a cypress tree in the middle of the fairway that is always a good target. The designers did all the players a great favor by leaving that tree.

PEBBLE BEACH GOLF LINKS: 18TH HOLE DIAGRAM

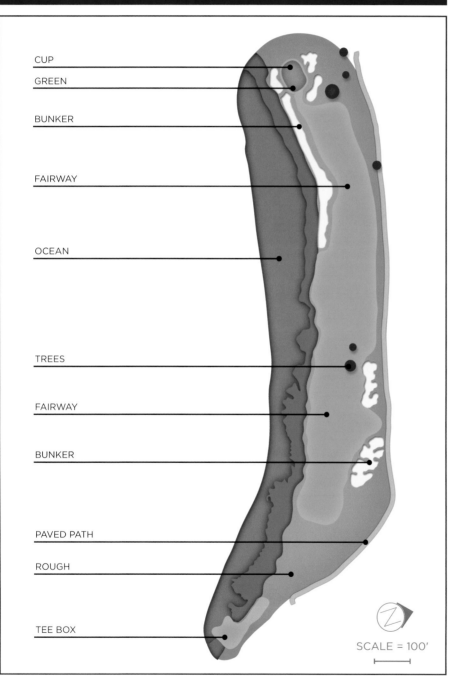

CUP

GREEN

BUNKER

FAIRWAY

OCEAN

TREES

FAIRWAY

BUNKER

PAVED PATH

ROUGH

TEE BOX

SCALE = 100'

OPPOSITE: *The coastline of the 18th hole at Pebble Beach Golf Links.*

"The second shot is much like the first. You're playing over the corner of the ocean. It's a dogleg left, and in the old days, you used to have a small strip of sand there buffering the ocean. Now there's a larger waste bunker and an ocean wall, so you are visually encouraged to play out farther to the right. If you're going to try to reach that green in two shots, you better be supremely confident and very aggressive. There's no room for error. You have to hit great shots to reach that green in 2.

"The smarter and more conservative play is to lay the ball up out of the right, leaving yourself 100 to 120 yards for your third shot. What I love about the hole is that the tee shot is hard and visually intimidating, and the second

"WHAT I LOVE ABOUT THE HOLE IS THAT THE TEE SHOT IS HARD AND VISUALLY INTIMIDATING, AND THE SECOND SHOT IS EQUALLY HARD AND INTIMIDATING WHETHER YOU'RE GOING FOR THE GREEN OR LAYING UP."

—PETER JACOBSEN

shot is equally hard and intimidating whether you're going for the green or laying up. If you're going for the green, it's all or nothing. And if you're laying up, you have to be very precise to avoid a huge tree that overhangs the right side of the green.

"The other intimidating factor is the wind. Whether it's the tee shot, the second or third shot, or the putts, wind can be gusting from all different directions. You are right on the edge of the ocean; there are no wind breaks, and no trees to stop it. If the wind gets blowing 20 to 25 miles an hour as it

usually does there, you're trying to hit a shot or a putt and the wind is moving you around. That's tough.

"It's a mind game. When you get to the 18th at Pebble Beach and you're one shot behind, you say to yourself, 'Hey, I can make a birdie here,' because you know the guy in the lead is going to get to that tee and say, 'Oh my gosh, how am I going to make a par?' Where you stand in the tournament dictates the attitude you're going to take into the hole. If you and I were just fooling around playing a casual round, we would think it's the most beautiful hole in the world and we'd have a great time trying to birdie it. But if you're in the lead in a tournament and that wind is blowing right to left and you're trying to slip a drive out there between the tree and the ocean, it's one of the most difficult and intimidating holes you'll ever play.

"If you polled tour players, two out of three would say that if they could only play one more round in their life, they would play at Pebble Beach. That speaks of the integrity of the design. The changes that have been made have protected the integrity of the course, which is fantastic. Arnold Palmer has done a fantastic job. And the 18th is still the greatest finishing par 5 in the game."

There is no more spectacular, go-for-it-at-your-peril finishing hole in all of golf than the 18th at Pebble Beach: a dogleg left along the edge of Carmel Bay with a landing area that fights the eye by running at an angle away from where the incoming shot must fly. Amazingly, the original architects missed it by a mile. When Jack Neville and Douglas Grant laid out the new Pebble Beach resort in 1919, the finishing hole was a pedestrian par 4, nothing to match the glamour of the seventeen holes before it. Thankfully, that was rectified in 1928 when two-time U.S. Amateur champion H. Chandler Egan and his

LEFT: *A view of the 18th hole during a wind-blown three-hour delay on the last day of the 2009 AT&T Pebble Beach National Pro-Am.*

design partner Robert Hunter reworked Pebble Beach and created the par-5 masterpiece that players see today.

According to U.S. Open champion and Hall of Fame broadcaster Ken Venturi, the hole "cannot be played timidly," and history has proved him correct. There is no room for bailouts. As 1948 Masters winner Claude Harmon once said, "If you're standing on that tee with the slightest lack of confidence in your swing, you might as well quit, because you're going to end up in the ocean."

Tom Watson understood that. In the 1982 U.S. Open, Watson had come to the 17th hole tied with Nicklaus, but after a miraculous chip-in from the back rough for a birdie, a shot still ranked among the greatest in the game's history, Watson came to the 18th with a one-shot lead. "A lot of people forget that I still had to play eighteen," Watson said. That was no easy bargain, especially holding a one-shot lead in the U.S. Open. But Watson was up to the task. He hit three perfect shots, and rolled in a short putt for birdie to clinch his first U.S. Open title by two shots.

Tiger Woods set a major championship record at Pebble Beach in 2000, winning the U.S. Open by fifteen shots in a display so spectacular that NBC announcer Roger Maltbie rightly said, "This is not a fair fight." Still, Tiger's tournament wasn't completely flawless. He hit one of his only poor shots of the week Saturday morning on the 18th as he was finishing the fog-delayed second round. When he pull-hooked his drive into the ocean, he slammed the driver into the turf. Despite his outburst, Woods got away with just a bogey on the hole and cruised on to victory.

While only a few tweaks have been made to the hole since 1928, the rocks and water look much closer now than they once did. That's because a new sea wall was created in 1998 after the El Niño floods destroyed much of the existing shoreline. The new erosion-proof wall gives the boundary a more angular and intimidating look. The latest renovations are far more subtle: In preparation for the 2010 U.S. Open, Arnold Palmer and his design team reshaped bunkers and restored the green surfaces to their original size and contour, especially on the 18th, where the green had become much smaller over the years. The changes give Pebble Beach a more classic look without changing the things that make it one of the most spectacular golf experiences in the world. As long as people love nature and continue to invent games to be played outdoors, spots like Pebble Beach will forever stimulate the senses and stir the soul.

ABOVE: *Golfers line up their putts on the 18th green during a practice round of the AT&T Pebble Beach National Pro-Am, February 3, 2003. The 18th hole featured two changes that year: a new tree at left that was transplanted from the first hole and a new bunker off the fairway.* **OPPOSITE:** *The 18th tee at Pebble Beach Golf Links.*

ACKNOWLEDGMENTS

Golfers are, by nature, an agreeable lot. They are the most approachable professional athletes, and in many ways the most enjoyable to be around. Jack Nicklaus, the greatest of his generation, remains a reporter's dream, an easy-to-reach superstar who always seems to have time for his fans and for anyone with an interesting question. I never saw him give an interview where he didn't finish by asking, "Do you have everything you need?" It's a question that rarely tumbles from the lips or even enters the minds of most modern public figures. For the greatest golfers in the game, returning calls and chatting about golf holes is commonplace, but no less appreciated. I thank them all.

No book is ever the sole property of the author. If everyone acknowledged all of those who made it possible for an idea to find its way onto the printed page, special libraries would have to be reserved for such lists. This book is no different. In addition to all the players who gave their time, I want to thank their staff and agents who helped facilitate many of the conversations. To my friends Doc Giffin, Rocky Hambric, Guy Kinnings, Adrian Mitchell, Scott Tolley, Alan Bullington, and Eddie Smith, my most gracious thanks. And to my wonderful editor Kjersti Egerdahl and everyone else at becker&mayer and Sellers Publishing, who shepherded this project, I can't thank you enough.

As always, nothing in life would be possible without the help and support of my loving wife Debbie and my children. I thank them every day, and it's still not enough.

— Steve Eubanks

1 CHERRY HILLS COUNTRY CLUB

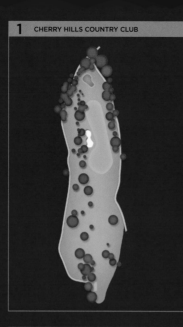

2 COURSE 3 AT MEDINAH COUNTRY CLUB

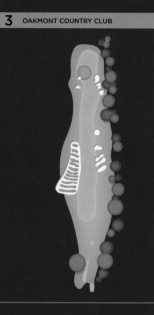

3 OAKMONT COUNTRY CLUB

7 OAK HILL COUNTRY CLUB

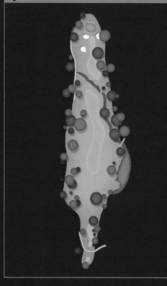

8 ROYAL TROON GOLF CLUB

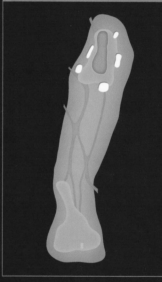

9 MUIRFIELD

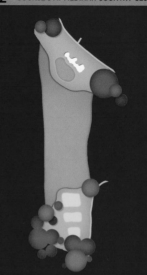

13 SHINNECOCK HILLS GOLF CLUB

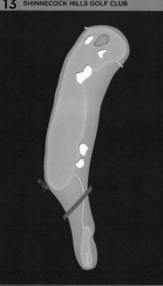

14 MUIRFIELD VILLAGE

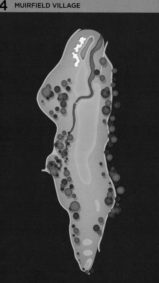

15 AUGUSTA NATIONAL GOLF CLUB

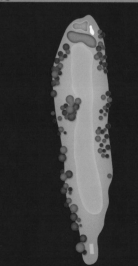

4 BETHPAGE BLACK COURSE	**5** PINEHURST NO. 2	**6** COMPOSITE COURSE AT ROYAL MELBOURNE GOLF CLUB

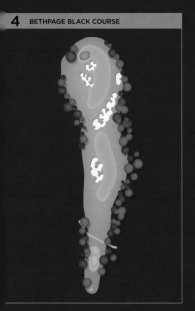 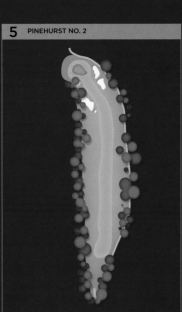 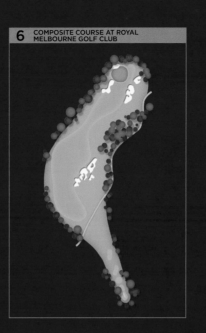

10 RIVIERA COUNTRY CLUB	**11** BALLYBUNION OLD COURSE	**12** AUGUSTA NATIONAL GOLF CLUB

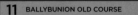

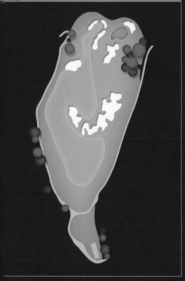 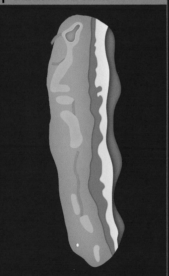 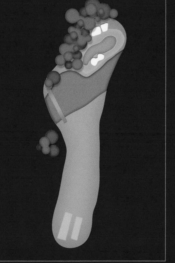

16 CYPRESS POINT CLUB	**17** THE OLD COURSE AT ST. ANDREWS	**18** PEBBLE BEACH GOLF LINKS

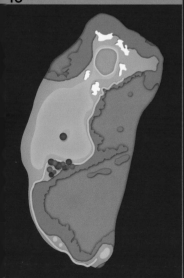 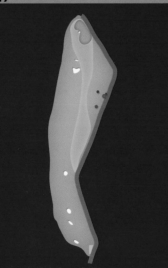

ABOUT THE AUTHOR

STEVE EUBANKS is a best-selling author and award-winning writer whose work has appeared in *Sports Illustrated*, *Golf Digest*, *Golf World*, *Golf Magazine*, *Golf for Women*, *T+L Golf*, the *Global Golf Post*, FoxSports.com, PGATour.com, and *USA Today*, among others. After spending his early career as a club professional and golf manager, he wrote the first unauthorized club history of Augusta National. He has since written more than thirty other books, including co-authorships with Arnold Palmer, Lou Jeff Gordon, Butch Harmon, and many more professional golfers. Steve was also the publishing consultant for the Royal and Ancient Golf Club at St. Andrews. He now lives in Peachtree City, Georgia, with his wife and children.

IMAGE CREDITS